Santa Clara Valley Library System
Mountain View Public Library
Santa Clara County Free Library
California

Alum Rock
Campbell
Cupertino
Gilroy
Los Altos

Milpitas { Calaveras
            Community Center
            Sunnyhills
Morgan Hill
Saratoga { Quito
            Village
Stanford-Escondido

Research Center-Cupertino
For Bookmobile Service, request schedule

Other Books by LEO LITWAK
    To the Hanging Gardens
    Waiting for the News

Other Books by HERBERT WILNER
    All the Little Heroes
    Dovisch in the Wilderness and
        Other Stories

college
days
in
earthquake
country

ordeal at San Francisco State

a personal record

ollege
days
in
earthquake
country

by LEO LITWAK
and HERBERT WILNER

RANDOM HOUSE · New York

ISBN: 0–394–47228–4
Library of Congress Catalog Card Number: 70–159355

Book design by Mary M. Ahern

Manufactured in the United States of America
by Haddon Craftsmen, Scranton, Penna.

9 8 7 6 5 4 3 2

FIRST EDITION

To **BENY WILNER**
and
To **ISAAC LITWAK**
still on the line

ACKNOWLEDGMENTS

I wish to express my gratitude to the Guggenheim Foundation for providing me with the resources to finish my part of this work and to undertake other writing.

Leo Litwak

The Soldier Walks Under The Trees
of the University

The walls have been shaded for so many years
By the green magnificence of these great lives
Their bricks are darkened till the end of time.
(Small touching whites in the perpetual
Darkness that saturates the unwalled world;   `
Saved from the sky by leaves, and from the earth by stone)
The pupils trust like flowers to the shades
And interminable twilight of these latitudes.

In our zone innocence is born in banks
And cultured in colonies the rich have sown:
The one is spared here what the many share
To write the histories that others are.
The oak escapes the storm that broke the reeds,
They read here; they read, too, of reeds,
Of storms; and are, almost, sublime
In their read ignorance of everything.

The poor are always—somewhere, but not here;
We learn of them where they and Guilt subsist
With Death and Evil: in books, in books, in books.
Ah, sweet to contemplate the causes, not the things!
The soul learns fortitude in libraries,
Enduring patience in another's pain,
And pity for the lives we do not change:
All that the world would be, if it were real.

When will the boughs break blazing from these trees,
The darkened walls float heavenward like soot?
The days when men say: "Where we look is fire—
The iron branches flower in my veins"?
In that night even to be rich is difficult,
The world is something even books believe,
The bombs fall all year long among the states,
And the blood is black upon the upturned leaves.
                                        —RANDALL JARRELL

The great problems are in the street.
                                        —NIETZSCHE

Troublemakers at San Francisco State College

After two decades of college teaching we had been in the grip of institutional habits which had little in common with our original professional impulses. That's not a unique condition. It doesn't happen only to college professors. Everyone gets tired of his work, and there is, no doubt, much greater reason for discontent among factory workers and salesmen and entrepreneurs and corporation executives. At least we had the advantage of doing our work in the midst of the young. We had the constant opportunity of rejuvenation. That was also our peril.

In the last few years, however, powerful currents of change had begun to loosen this grip. And located where we were—in the place where innovations had immediate and strong impact—we were especially vulnerable. San Francisco State College was at the epicenter of cultural earthquakes. It was home base for the beatniks and, afterward, for the hippies. It was, at the same time, a streetcar college with broad working-class representation. And it was directly in the path of the political storms that buffeted the Bay Area.

Some professors knew almost from the beginning of those years where they stood. Some enthusiastically surrendered when the new life beckoned, and they doffed academic garb in favor of exotic colors and shapes. Hair came down and beards flourished. A few professors journeyed to Big Sur and discovered how to release feelings and establish informal connections with their students. There were other professors who sought to invigorate the faculty by involving it in the labor movement. A few discovered a new source of energy in direct association with militant students. All these efforts to reexamine academic traditions seemed accompanied by a willingness to scrap them all if they were found wanting.

On the other hand, there were some in the established faculty, those with decades of service in the system, who rejected any deviation from the standards of their own graduate-school training, fearing that it would lead to degeneration and decay.

The bulk of the faculty, however—among whom we reckoned ourselves—didn't know where they stood. In the year preceding the San Francisco State strike, those of us who were most confused were buffeted by contradictions, alternately dreading the threatened radical innovations and seeing them as potentially revivifying. We, in particular, no longer had the sense of choosing our lives. We were immobilized by conflicting desires: the need to retain those innocent hopes with which we had come to teaching by narrowing our vision, and the need to open our eyes and notice what was happening even if that should undermine our professional lives.

By the fall of 1968, after a year of assault by the SDS and other essentially white radical parties, we weren't entirely intact, but we still hoped that our troubles would eventually end and "normalcy" be restored. While we witnessed police brutality we understood the tactical objectives in provoking the police, and we could conclude that police victims had not been innocent. We felt we might be able to weather the storms by remaining cynical and ironical and never committing ourselves to a stand.

The black students, however, were to make such aloofness

impossible. They would not let us evade our conflicts. They were to pry beneath our irony and set loose hatreds and fears and compassion. The theater they were to perform with the police would involve us more powerfully than had the white radicals. The Blacks would compel us to acknowledge truths about the way we lived. Indeed, the strike declared by the Black Students Union at San Francisco State College on November 6, 1968, was to initiate a mode of racial confrontation that would in the next year sweep the nation's campuses. It was farewell to our dreams of a campus sanctuary.

If a change in consciousness was due, we hardly welcomed it. The readjustment threatened to be too painful. We would have preferred that trouble pass us over as the angel of death passed over the houses of the chosen people. And we could have regarded ourselves as having been chosen by an elaborate process which discarded the unworthy and raised us finally to an invulnerable tenured status. But it's not easy accepting the bounty of grace while others are dreadfully plagued. And the Blacks wouldn't allow us to be contented.

The year 1968 was an election year and our campus was visited by Eldridge Cleaver, nominated by the Peace and Freedom Party to be President of the United States. Cleaver summoned the huge crowd to seize power. Reds, Blacks, Browns, Yellows, students, even faculty, he said, should seize power. It was a message that Black Panther Minister of Education, George Murray, also delivered, standing on a table in the commons dining room at San Francisco State College, indicating that the campus revolution would be armed. There was talk of guns. On November 5, Stokely Carmichael addressed the assembled Blacks in the Main Auditorium to inspire them for the imminent strike. The next day groups of Blacks raided classrooms, and the police were summoned and the campus was shut down. Our ramparts were under attack. So what did we do? We joined the large minority of faculty that belonged to the teachers' union and we went on strike. Instead of repelling the forces that assaulted us, we joined them. We walked a picket line alongside members of the Black Students Union and the Third World Liberation Front and the SDS. It was an unstable coalition.

We operated within the context of a union, but what did we have in common with working men? Some of us who had never donned a pair of work pants except perhaps in a play bellowed, "Scab!" at colleagues who crossed our lines. Scholars yelled, "Fuck you!"

At the beginning of that school year we had never imagined that within a few weeks we would be among the "handful of troublemakers" denounced by Governor Reagan as responsible for the campus strife. We anticipated the usual cops-and-students encounter. We never imagined that by the end of the semester we would be labor union veterans hefting picket signs, trudging along the periphery of our place of work in aimless circles through a miserable winter.

It was a revelation to discover that we were among the bad guys, damned by eighty percent of the public, to whom S.I. Hayakawa appeared—however implausibly to us—as some kind of messiah. We were the target of the state's overwhelming power. Governor Reagan, whose idea of campus life was perhaps shaped by old times at Eureka College, meant to solve contradictions by brute surgery. He meant to excise the troublemakers and cast them back into the street. He found the surgeon he wanted in Hayakawa, who had long advocated, at the very least, strong medicine.

We were no fools. We knew where the power was. Why did we risk a style of life to which we were attached for a cause about which we had misgivings? And one that was unlikely to succeed?

That's the story of this book. We have deliberately chosen to be personal. We hope to discover a generic condition by examining the process which led us to strike. We suspect that our lives reflect those American myths which govern both our streets and our schools. So we begin our account at the very beginning, watching cowboy movies on Saturday afternoon, preparing for war, getting the proper angle on the ball carrier during a football game, hard times in a Brooklyn ghetto, our lives on the street before we arrive at the Golden Country of the Youth where, in another time, we might have expected our lives to be serenely, blessedly, absent-minded.

LEO LITWAK
HERBERT WILNER

November 6, 1970

CONTENTS

college
days
in
earthquake
country

After the war I decided to be a wise and secure man, and embarked on a college career. I found that I could be secure but at the penalty of not being wise. Academic subjects and academic protocol were rarely concerned with cardinal matters and if the great issues of our time were to be engaged, it would have to be off-campus. I reconciled myself to the fact that this was the price I had to pay for my good life among the young, for my pleasant work and my safe harbor.

LEO LITWAK

1 · the safe harbor

LEO LITWAK

The walls of my schoolroom were placarded with the bromides of Benjamin Franklin. We learned the virtues of thrift, delayed pleasure, respect for authority. But even at the level of the primary school there was a rival wisdom being taught in the schoolyard. Our texts weren't drawn from Benjamin Franklin, but rather from the cowboy instructors who taught us each Saturday afternoon that the shoot-out was the final solution to all inequities. The cowboy was no Benjamin Franklin. The model offered by the cowboy hero wasn't mercantile. You didn't wait for orderly process to relieve your misery and bring earned pleasure. The gun did the job immediately and that was especially attractive to children for whom the penny-saving route must seem infinitely frustrating. So in the schoolyard and in the street a cowboy morality prevailed.

The youth of our Detroit ghetto line up outside the Dexter Theater. We are schoolmates. We share a common cuisine, religion, and nightmare. Hitler's grand design, which no one seems able to resist, includes gobbling up our Dexter Avenue community and spewing it forth as ashes. When we listen to the news at home and observe the desperate concentration of our parents who are still intimately connected to Europe we are frightened, because our parents see no way out. It is perfectly conceivable to them—since they have been on stage when history was made—that we may suffer catastrophes without afterward receiving justice. It is no pleasure listening to the news over the home radio.

But Saturday afternoon at the Dexter Theater is different.

There's not an adult in the crowd, except the theater manager. Even the ushers and the operators of the candy counter are young people. And we handle the news in our own fashion. When a flourish of brass introduces the *Fox Movietone News* and the lights dim and the cozy thunder of all the children in our neighborhood slowly muffles, we settle down joyfully to the sight of Adolph Hitler walking the Siegfried Line. What raspberries and exuberant abuse. Together we reduce the devil to comic size. We cheer the huge jaw and cocky grin of President Roosevelt. Mussolini, mincing down a line of soldiers in a funny cap and high boots, a hand braced at his waist, his elbow extended, we hoot off the screen. If on Saturday afternoon the newsreel is followed by a cowboy flick, we are momentarily relieved of nightmare by the illusion of cowboy justice.

My platoon was in reserve, stationed in a gulley outside a German village that our company assaulted. We crouched against the banks of the gulley to avoid sniper fire. A GI from an advance platoon returned to our area marching behind two German prisoners. One was tall and blond. The second prisoner was very young and frail. The prisoners marched before the American captor with their hands raised. The GI stopped. He aimed, fired, missed at a distance of ten yards. The prisoners continued marching and didn't look back. Perhaps I imagined the GI meant only to scare them. Otherwise why didn't I protest what then happened? The next shot knocked the young prisoner flat. The older one continued marching, his hands still raised high, still not turning. I muttered, "Oh, don't," before he, too, was shot. The GI only briefly considered what he had done. He didn't look at us— forty men on the banks who witnessed the scene. He returned to the front, his rifle loosely held at the ready. No one spoke of the murder. A short time later the village was taken and we entered it. Houses burned, fired by chemical mortars. A drunken tanker stood on the stairs of a burning house, one hand holding a bottle of wine, the other used to aim his piss into the street. Our platoon took over a fine house. We found sausages and preserves in the cellar. I saw a GI pursue a chicken with a bayonet. Four of us sprawled in a feather bed, our boots on, still in harness, and the murdered German soldiers were entirely dismissed from mind.

After twenty-five years I vaguely recall the older man. The back of his neck was weathered red and deeply creased. I can't visualize the younger one except to recall that he was slight, gray-clad and wore an overseas cap. The older man plodded ahead as if he still marched in ranks. Perhaps terror numbed him to dying. Perhaps he was rubbed out even before the bullet struck. Otherwise how could he continue his robot-like march? These weren't the only executions I saw. And many soldiers have told me of similar scenes they witnessed. Decent, amiable American boys committed murder. I don't put myself in the shoes of the dead men. I refuse to walk alongside the plodding German, trying to guess what the stolid GI had in mind. I accept these dead men as mere "extras." I manage to turn war into a combat movie. The movies were after all accurate reflections—not of historical events, but of how men are inclined to distort them. It's possible—just as Hollywood instructed us—to transact death wholesale, in cold blood, and not be affected. Once the battle is over and the army ritual is resumed, what really happened becomes irrelevant. Even combat troops end up going to cowboy movies. And in time they even believe mawkish fantasies, forgetting murders witnessed or committed, forgetting the weariness of trench life which they had once believed unbearable. They are ready for peace. They are prepared to become American Legionnaires. The cowboy myth which had been dispelled by combat wins out in the end. General Patton with his ivory-handled six-guns in twin holsters presents the authorized version of the Noble Warrior. Hollywood is more powerful than the experience it invalidates.

That's only true for most men. I discovered that there were serious shortcomings to the cowboy way of doing business. Like many other ex-GI's, I returned to the campus after the war. We separated from the street people with whom we had shared a public school experience and the myth of a cowboy hero.

I left the battlefields of Europe for the campuses of the Midwest, and in a surprisingly short time the experience of war seemed incredible. I chose a path that would conduct me to a safe harbor.

There are no monsters on campus—at least not the sort who do wholesale business in murder and even merchandise the by-products, such as the gold from teeth, hair, shoes, spectacles, wedding rings, everything that can be redeemed from soap and ashes. No one starves on campus. There are no massacres. We exclude our experience of man as cannibal, pervert, murderer. The campus aims to perfect that version of man which defines him as a rational animal. Academic language aims for nice sounds and precise distinctions. At least it once did. There was a time when the language was so demanding that when we talked philosophy we could only formulate trivial cases. We were confined to tables and chairs and other furniture.

The experience of the war didn't fit anywhere into the curriculum. I was both relieved by that exclusion and at the same time uncertain of the value of any truths not grounded in the battlefield. The inertia of campus life resists direct acquaintance with battlefields. We are moved from orientation to commencement through a variety of grades, and aspire to status on terms set by the hierarchy. We are judged en route by faculty who are to us what officers are to enlisted men. We are systematically confirmed as we move up each rung. At the end, if we are especially graced, we enter the academy as lowly officers. By this time, we have parted from our cowboy fantasies, have lost all but the vaguest recollections of war, and instead we dream of high status and academic glory.

There were occasions when being an undergraduate realized other childhood dreams that the movies had nurtured. I mean those grade B college movies starring Tom Brown or Tim Holt. The campus was a childhood place with a transparent rationale. In fact, I sometimes felt that the best part of college was not its intellectual demands, but its childish rituals. Sometimes, living in a kid's world, I could resent those who tried to undermine it, zealots who wanted us to establish connections with the streets.

Caught in an equivocation, I couldn't dismiss the hoopla of fraternity hazing, or Saturday football games, or the charm of long-legged coeds who seemed as inaccessible to me as fairy-tale princesses. At the same time, I couldn't accept a mode so alien to my experience. We had once commanded *Fräuleins*, not even troubling to say "hello" or "good-by." Yet in the presence of the coed we were once again virginal and timid.

Why deny the grace of those college girls? Why resist the cheerleader? Why shrink from the childish artifice that had contrived campus traditions? Was it artifice? Was it unreal? Were we obliged to recall the smell of blood whenever we were distracted from the grimmer human possibilities?

Wasn't it the heart of the Hobbesian wisdom that whatever lends life its grace is unnatural or contrived? So what if the curriculum reflected nothing about war? So what if it had no inherent logic, and was simply the by-product of established interests? Its main function was to initiate us into a system whose invented structure was the only one we had.

What continues to amaze and depress me is that I could so quickly and thoroughly lose sight of my experience and accept instead a mythic, infantile, Hollywood version of my life. It was very hard for me to escape the authority of the movies.

And so I become a teacher of philosophy, a very uneasy one. Why did I go to philosophy? Perhaps because I hoped it would reconcile my practice with my experience. Like all novices, I imagined the answers, or at least the questions, were located there. After only slight familiarity, I was ready like Hume to consign all books of metaphysics to the flames. Perhaps in search of ultimate questions I had to enter a realm of essences or ideas or forms. But the argument, once apprehended, had no effect on the way I conducted my life, only on the way I talked. Come to think of it, the way I talked did affect my life. In class, for instance, speaking in the guise of Leibniz or Kant or Spinoza, I felt myself committed to a priestly, arcane language. To return to the vernacular after class—as though the academic language only had utility during class time—was an act I considered hypocritical. So I began talking like a professor even out of class. In a way, that solved other problems. The college authorities didn't favor student-faculty intimacy unless the connection was represented as paternal. When I began teaching, I had only a few years' advantage on the youngest of my students. Some older ones antedated me by a generation. My oracular tone helped keep them at arm's length. That solved the problem even though my own inclination was to embrace, not shove away. We were—I now see—oriented to the last two weeks of school, when tests were administered and grades rendered. I was in the position of a magistrate and I had to remain impartial. Yet I found the students often closer to my perceptions than were my colleagues. I tried to resolve the difficulty by becoming a wise, avuncular man. Still in my twenties, that was no easy task.

St. Louis, where I first taught, was a Jim Crow town. Movies, restaurants, housing, schools were all segregated. Washington University admitted Blacks only to a few departments of the graduate school.

Several of my students in 1952 joined a new organization named CORE. They invited me to attend CORE demonstrations. I did so reluctantly, thinking my students naive. They didn't know the scary American possibilities I had studied up close on the European battlefields. A couple dozen of us, white and black, went to a downtown cafeteria at suppertime. A black lady took a position at the head of the serving line. The rest of us filled our trays and stood behind her. When she was refused service, we refused to advance. No one could pass us. The manager advised us in a hushed tone that he didn't want trouble. He whispered that he would phone the police if we didn't leave. He said he would be delighted to serve any race, any nationality. He wasn't a bigot, but he would be driven out of business if he served Blacks. If all other cafeterias served Blacks, he would be delighted to receive them. However, he refused to be integrated when his competition was not. From a balcony above the serving line, a white lady dumped sugar on our line. It rained down on the black lady. She flinched, but kept her place. We had been instructed to be nonviolent and not respond to abuse. The white lady leaned over the balcony

and poured sugar, and she looked as if she had an appetite
to eat us alive. She would as soon have poured molten lead.
She guarded her fortress by all available means. I had no
inclination to be violent. It surprised me that I was unnerved.
I'd been adequate on battlefields. But the hillbillies were
then on my side.

The more serious attraction of academic life—at least in the
liberal arts, where I knew it best—was the promise of a detached and entire view of experience. The wise man who is
the culmination of the academic condition is freed of bondage to the here and now. His passionate self is under control
and he finds joy in the contemplative life.

But I took no pleasure in the transcendental language and
the speculative mode which still prevailed after the war.
Logical positivism had arrived to threaten the rule of gentle-
men. It was a tough doctrine and it suited my mood and my
experience. The positivist movement attracted students who
were too skeptical to buy the "poetry" of metaphysical discourse and preferred the deflated language of operational-
ism. The positivist criterion of testability, which insisted that
meaningful discourse be grounded in hard physical fact, was
a relief from windy speculation. What had been passing as
moral philosophy, for instance, often seemed like pious advice of the Benjamin Franklin variety, elaborately delivered
by men of quite modest experience.

I felt liberated by the positivist language, which had no
moral pretensions. I was even attracted by the mechanism of
an artificial language, formulated in accordance with exact
rules and limited vocabularies. Every argument conducted
in these barren languages could be unambiguously certified
as valid or invalid, and that was a refreshing contrast to the
lush speculations of Establishment prose.

Also important for my frame of mind, the positivists offered a strong justification for differentiating our professional
obligations from our civil ones. As citizens we expressed our
moral commitments. As professional philosophers we were
concerned with cognitive statements that were morally neutral, and therefore we could stay out of wars.

I joined three other members of the faculty in circulating
a petition for the admission of Blacks to the university. The
chancellor was, at the time, Arthur Holly Compton, the Nobel laureate who supervised cracking the atom. We made
ourselves nervous imagining how our bold stand might provoke the engineering and the business faculty. Though our
chairman believed in our cause, he suggested that we not
rock the boat. We talked ourselves into watering down the
petition. We, the undersigned, advised the chancellor that
should he support the admission of Negroes to Washington
University, we would support him. The majority of the faculties of humanities and sciences signed the petition. Almost no
one from the engineering and business schools signed. The
chancellor accepted our petition benignly. While himself
sympathetic, he feared that the community at large would
oppose the move even though the campus might be ready for
it. He acknowledged that we had acted with the best intentions.

We thanked the chancellor and retreated, having done
very little to relieve human bondage. The chancellor could
have been right. It might have been dangerous to permit
black students on campus. Black men weren't even allowed
on the same battlefield with us. During the war I saw them
in the Quartermaster Corps. I saw them working in the mess
halls and supply rooms and motor pools and driving garbage
trucks. When I suggested to my white buddies that black
men were human too, I was called a "nigger lover." A ser-

geant trudged alongside me during a training march and said, "Know what a Jew is, Litwak? A nigger turned inside out." My buddies were real killers, as I've already observed. It confused me that they were also decent, amiable, apple-pie-loving American boys capable of kind and gentle acts. They didn't see niggers as rational animals. They saw them as eligible for slaughter. And some felt the same about Jews. I, too, thanked our Nobel prize-winning chancellor for accepting our petition. Two years later the Supreme Court ended segregation at the university by fiat. The community at large accepted the decision without any fuss.

I enthusiastically embraced positivism in my teaching. I favored ruthless surgery on all systems which pretended to offer definitive answers to the ultimate questions. I believed in the nobility of my calling. I was often excited by elegant argument. My goal wasn't money, so I didn't object when I began teaching at a salary of less than three thousand dollars. Nor did I feel exploited when seven years later, married, with a child, no longer in my twenties, my earnings had only increased to five-thousand dollars.

I knew what other advantages I enjoyed. My work seemed preferable to the drudgery to which others were condemned. The campus was lovely. The students were lovely. We who were junior faculty members were subject each year to retention decisions. All power was vested in deans and chairmen and senior faculty. Senior faculty were in those days old-timers who feared that the influx of ex-GI's would erode traditions and curricular empires that had once seemed unalterable. The American college had changed little to reflect our new experience. Now the inundation sponsored by the GI Bill doomed a way of life. I had no impulse to rock the boat, being a Depression child myself. I had once thought a guaranteed salary of fifty-dollars a week marked the well-to-do from the poor. Furthermore, in a violent world, the academy was a serene place.

Money isn't everything. Don't rock the boat.

In 1951 a friend of mine took leave from the Philosophy Department to head a research project for the Navy. Following the election of Eisenhower, the Navy advised all civilian heads of research projects to resign in order that military personnel could replace them. My friend was warned that if he didn't cooperate by resigning, he would be subject to a security check. Joe McCarthy was in the saddle. Subversives were hunted everywhere, and the campus was a favorite hunting ground. We were safe if we didn't rock the boat. We could keep our noses clean by avoiding all political activity that was outside regular party organizations. We could also swear, whenever asked, that we were loyal Americans and belonged to no subversive organization. My friend was no boat-rocker. But he was in the way of an organization that was so eager to hunt the beast that it invented subversives. My friend was duly charged as a security risk. He sent me a photostat of the charges which concerned his activities as a faculty member at Washington University, and asked me to gather evidence in his support. He was charged with being a campus adviser to the Student Committee for the Admission of Negroes. This committee was said to contain among its executive board certain individuals who belonged to an organization listed as subversive by the Attorney General's office. I checked. My friend was not an adviser to SCAN. That honor belonged to the campus Y.M.C.A. director. There were other charges of a like kind, all trivial, all baseless. It took my friend one year to clear himself. He used up most of his resources. His reputation was damaged. Why should a man have to worry about his reputation? Why should he be careful not to rock the boat? Professors were not in high demand at the time. There were dozens ready to replace anyone who fell out, despite the miserable compensation. My friend came from a poor family. He had also known the bite of depression. The threat of being unemployed was powerful. We didn't rock the boat. We bided our time, hoping that someday we'd have our innings.

Yet, when my generation finally came to power, we had so long accepted the system that we introduced only modest changes. The design of the university remained basically unaltered. We toyed with the curriculum. Enrollment increased. But neither in content nor in form was a college education substantially different from what it had been at the turn of the century. Logical positivism was absorbed into the Establishment as were succeeding philosophical fashions.

We surely didn't mean to rock the boat, even though it was so swamped with bilge it needed overturning.

I skip all further personal history to arrive at the event which is the subject of this book, the "strike" that began November 6, 1968, at San Francisco State College.

I heard a black youth call the college president a "fat pig" in front of the assembled faculty.

I heard a tall Mexican-American in a rumpled army field jacket, boots, red scarf—uncombed beard and hair giving him the look of a buccaneer—tell the cowed faculty and administration, "No one but the Third World people have the right to determine what their education will be. We don't want anyone telling us what we need or how to present our demands."

Their demands were designed to overturn the boat.

Open enrollment for all Third World peoples.

A black leader addressing a convocation of the faculty and

student body warned us that we were involved in a revolution. "The guides and rules of the college as indicated in the catalog should be destroyed. Then we can begin to deal with the kind of education that influences our lives. Education in this country originally was designed for the elite. We are not members of the elite and this education is not relevant to us." These weren't the elite. The street people we had left behind in high school or before had breached our fortress. "We warn you that if you don't move over, we will move over you."

They raided classrooms and jostled students and professors and forced classes to end. Bombs went off in the Administration Building, the Creative Arts Building, the Psychology Building. The house of an acting dean was bombed. One professor who opposed the Black Studies Program had the tires of his car slashed. A bomb was found outside his office door.

I saw a boy wearing a Hayakawa blue arm band knocked down by a leader of the Black Students Union.

The president of the college wearily confessed to his assembled constituency, "I am trying to be my own president. I have often been pushed to the edge and this has made me ineffective."

Despite our resolve, the campus had become a battlefield.

A black dean, standing defiantly with the Third World, said: "We will never return to normal. The real world is a world in which we take risks. Growing up is painful. Victims, not the oppressors, must set the timetable. If the oppressor sets the timetable, he'll stay with this trick another three hundred years." He made clear what he considered to be a relevant education. It wasn't Aristotle. "More education has gone on since the strike began than in the whole six years I was a student here."

A robot voice blared from a loudspeaker: "Everyone disperse and don't get involved in the actions that are taking place. Please go to your classes."

I see a wild-haired student in blue denims and a red bandanna wrestling with plain-clothes men in the middle of the crowd. They haul him toward the Business and Social Science Building, where I have my office. The crowd swarms around, girls shrieking, others yelling "pig." I see white-faced students trying to rescue the one who has been arrested. A plain-clothes man pulls out a pistol and I'm afraid the students don't realize the danger. I hear glass shatter. I hear a pistol shot a few yards from where I'm standing. Students flee past me. A chubby girl, a radical leader, races by in panic. The blue-jacketed policeman comes fast down the walk without his prisoner, still harassed by the crowd. His pistol is out. He seems both infuriated and frightened. The students pursuing him are also frightened.

I haven't felt this kind of shock since the battlefields of Europe. We are on the edge of murder.

The police line up, tensed, moving forward with threatening twitches of riot clubs gripped in both hands, visors down. I see them flail away. I see students on the ground, gripping bloody heads, while cops still flail away.

A black leader, addressing the assembled School of Humanities faculty, says, "These demands aren't the last. Even if you met all our demands this would only be the beginning." He tells us that revolution is coming. The constantly repeated phrase that eventually becomes a national cliché is "relevant education." "Maybe," this black leader tells us, "we'll have to reevaluate everything we've been taught. Maybe we'll have to burn Aristotle."

All my laborious struggle with the Metaphysics and the Physics up in smoke?

At the end of the year, I went out on strike with more than two hundred colleagues, partly in support of the student objectives.

The new president, Hayakawa, accused the striking faculty of being essentially bored with teaching and deriving excitement from the student revolutionaries. While he meant this accusation to be damning, he himself exuberantly confessed after the bloodiest day of the strike, "This has been the most exciting day since my tenth birthday, when I rode a roller coaster for the first time." It was a callous statement and yet both his indictment and his confession reported what we had all experienced—a new energy that changed our connections to each other and our institition. I taught my students at my home without pay. And never was teaching more joyful.

Others considered me a professor who wrote; I thought of myself as a writer who taught. I lived an academic man's life, loved teaching, was committed to San Francisco State, but reserved for myself, out of boyhood memories, a disdain for academic nonsense. Sometimes, on campus, I thought I was arguing against such absurdities in fairly plain talk. But it never occurred to me that I could be, in any of my objections, anything but a reasonable man. I ordered my life everywhere by the rules of the game.

HERBERT WILNER

2 · street & campus: rules of the game

HERBERT WILNER

At the union meetings during the college crisis, I grew tired of being told by so many others who I was: an intellectual, a laborer, a professor, a liberal, a radical, a pawn, a hero, an equivocator, a potential fink. At one such meeting we were to vote on a policy toward off-campus teaching. A few of the leaders of the Black Students Union were there to persuade us against teaching anywhere. They stood together at the rear of the crowded room, silently tolerating all the long-winded professorial rhetoric that any debate among us always produced. Occasionally they whispered to each other. Sometimes one of them would single out a faculty member and begin a staring contest. Always alert to our awareness of them, their gestures, even their silences, seemed calculated.

When they finally spoke up, their rhetoric was familiar. There was to be no off-campus teaching—a strike was a strike. They mixed gun threats against our executive committee with passionate statements about the origin of their revolutionary struggle. We, as whites, were once more a part of the problem or a part of the solution, and the solution did not have to do with our jobs, our salaries, our middle-class lives or our *bull*shit liberalism, and least of all with our concern for white students who worried about their semester grades. We who were so used to lecturing were now being lectured to as though we were the Freshman class at the orientation assembly. George Murray, the BSU leader and Black Panther official, whose recent militancy had locked horns with the State of California and thus made for the

public beginning of the present crisis, leaned forward and
angrily swept the room with his arm. He was dressed in an
army field jacket and wore the habitual sunglasses. He reminded us of the source of our luxurious verbosities. We
didn't really know the black man's struggles. We didn't know
the ghetto. We didn't know poverty.

In the remembered years of my boyhood in Brooklyn, we
move eleven times. We follow in the Depression after my
immigrant father's storekeeper disasters, all of us dragged by
his fatal knack for barging into failure, until even his renew-
als of bitter and delusionary optimism for *this* new store and
another new neighborhood peter out in welfare checks
called Relief. I get used to packing and unpacking, to making
friends and leaving them, even to the new places which I am
to call home, house, rooms. They are always tenement apart-
ments or rooms behind or above the store, the familiar housing of the poor: roaches, mice, sometimes rats, and crowded
quarters. In the winter I sometimes sleep in clothes. I can't
believe that I'm "deprived," for nothing in the neighborhood
provides a sense of lives different from my own. There is no
TV. The radio can't make our envies visual. There's seldom
money for the movies, which belong, anyway, like the fun-
nies and anything I read for school, to the world of make-
believe. The places in which we live are always and only a
little bit better or a little bit worse than the place we had
before.

But I never get used to the new schools. The institution in
a foreign place is always a threat. There are mazes of bewildering and frightening regulations and conditions in each
new school: how and where you line up in the morning,
where you go to lunch, what you can play in the schoolyard,
when you can talk, when you can't, what you wear for assem-

bly, where the toilet is and how you get permission to go there. The classroom full of staring kids that I come to in the middle of the term is a trial, and the new teacher might turn out a witch who will soon inhabit my nightmares. It is in the class on my first day that I get my premonitory sense of what my life is to be like out of the school as well as in it. I learn the nature of names, and even before I am to know "Italian" and "Jew," I know there will be a difference for me in a class full of Nicks and Vincents and Tonys and Tessies, and one full of Sauls and Irvings and Melvins and Glorias.

I am eight or nine and we move to Fulton Street under the El that has since been torn down. I don't need to wait for the names to know my differences. We are in Bedford-Stuyvesant, and in the new class I am one of three or four white kids. My family lives behind the store darkened by the El, in small windowless rooms where everything rattles when the train goes by. I remember only moments inside the patterns of this time. As on that day when I come out of the back rooms and stand in the doorway of the store, listening to the raised voices of my father and a black customer, who gesticulates wildly with his arms. I notice how short my father is. He shouts that he will call the police, and as I stand there trembling I make wordless prayers for the appearance of such a policeman. He will be white, and he will be on our side even as my white teacher in school is already on my side.

I can also remember an occasion when I am on the street a few blocks from the store and three black boys talk me out of a coin I have. Perhaps I tell them of the nickel or dime because I am afraid they will otherwise search me. They don't touch me; they don't even threaten me. They merely talk for it, and I deliver it to them. They don't need to frighten me to know I am frightened of them. This is their street, in their neighborhood. It is littered with the broken glass of whiskey bottles and the rags of discarded, dirty clothes. In summer it smells everywhere of sweat and urine, and everywhere and always there are the cursing, unpredictable adults who loiter on the streets or stand at open windows. And in these streets the black boys of my age, flashing smiles, walk free and easy, while I take to learning the names of baseball players as I stay in the rooms behind the store after school and listen to the radio.

When we move thereafter to Brownsville, on the edge of a vast Jewish ghetto, where it begins to merge with a black neighborhood, I make friends with a black boy. I go with him after school one day to where he lives, a block from my house. There are steps with an iron railing leading to a glass front door, but we go around and under them to a latched wooden door and through it into a dark, windowless room. His mother sits on an uncovered mattress on a cotbed. His father is in the room and he stares at me and says nothing. He wears no shirt over the long-sleeved underwear with dirty cuffs. In the room itself there is that odor I have smelled in their hallways and the piss-corners of the schoolyards. I feel strange and frightened in this cellar room where I imagine anything and everything can happen. I have no idea where that sense comes from. Perhaps I imagine that their cellar-poor is poorer than my tenement-poor, but that of itself should not make for a picture of anything I need to dread. I remember that for a while we play with a board game, on the cracked linoleum floor, and then I leave, grateful to be going home.

It never occurs to me to imagine what my classmate would feel had we played in my house. I would like now to believe he too would have been intimidated by the strange odors of my mother's cooking and by the spoken Yiddish. It would relieve me of believing that even as a boy I was what the BSU leaders today call racist, deriving my white anxieties from more than strangeness, from that subtle conviction even at nine that black people could commit deeds a white would find unthinkable. It would help me to believe that the profoundest differences between races merely start at the skin. It is all brutally difficult, and it goes finally beyond skin and poverty. Without end we multiply the consequences of our little confusions and our essential simplicities. We learn our fears so much earlier than we learn how to guard against them in the simple name of love and decency. And most often we will, in our minds at least, flee if we can from what we so early learned to fear.

The young man in my office was a married graduate student who came to explain why he had not yet turned in any stories for his writing course. Unlike most of my students, he wore a sports jacket and tie, and his hair was neat. He had a self-effacing smile and gentle eyes in an intelligent and strained New England face. There was no lingo in his talk; nothing was "groovy," "beautiful," "in a bag," or "uptight." He had just returned from the small town in his home state where he had once more been called before the local draft board. A good part of his first month of the semester had been spent preparing the written statements to document his conscientious objection on moral grounds to the war in Vietnam. He didn't say so, but I imagined much of his time had also been spent in agonizing over the outcome.

"What will you do if they turn you down?"

"I don't know," he said, shrugging, smiling against himself. "It's been going on for two years. I have to go back again in May. I have to write more statements. I suppose I'll have to go to jail. Or leave the country. I can't go to that war. I won't."

Leave the country, or go to jail. This young man (and there have been so many others in my office to tell the same story), by his looks and manners and intentions for his life, created the image I myself used to make when I was only a boy, in order to seize the myth in the history I needed for the country I lived in and in which my parents had not been born. I could not have gotten it from my own life. It came rather from resounding phrases in books and speeches. "I swear eternal enmity against all forms of tyranny over the mind of man." "With malice toward none, with charity for all . . ." "I hear America singing . . ." Leave the country, or go to jail. And all I did was sigh, and shake loose a compassionate look, and say, "It's rough." And think to myself about the tyranny of circumstances, in which I had not in my own life had to endure such choices.

When we began to talk about his writing, the student admitted to a growing affection for Beckett. He was reading *Watt* and howling with laughter. "I suppose it comes out of my own predicament," he said. "That and other things. When I was at Berkeley I was involved a lot in the demonstrations. Now I can't even think about them seriously. I think it's all funny. Everything is just so damned funny." He smiled at me, reticently and hopelessly.

I am a month or two past eighteen and on my way to Grand Central Palace for my army physical. I am among the oldest in the gang I have been running with since the age of twelve, when we stopped moving, and so among the first to be called. I go to the physical with mixed feelings. I want to imagine myself at the service of and even a hero in the great national cause that will rescue the world from Hitler and avenge the day of infamy at Pearl Harbor. On the other hand, I am anxious about the interruption of my daily life, which has

nothing to do with the streetcar college I attend or preparations for a career. I don't want to leave my neighborhood
friends.

At this time I live in the new security of a permanent
address. We no longer move. We live above a store in rooms
a little bit better than those we have come from, and in a
neighborhood much better than any in which we have lived
before. In my adolescence I live mainly on the streets, and
in the schoolyards, and in the gyms, where my new life rip-
ens. I am aided by an accidental gift: I can play ball. On those
streets, it means citizenship. Things get even better for me.
The gang becomes formal: we have a club, and I am forever
president; we have uniformed teams, and I am forever captain. Perhaps it comes to me because, even as an adolescent,
I can no more keep my mind from expressing distinctions
than another boy's fist can stay at his side when a dose of
adrenalin spurts from his gland. At thirteen and fourteen I
am already full of "if's" and "but's" and other such adolescent
teeth-grinders as "It's not that simple," or "I think we ought
to think about it some more," and "It's not the same thing
as . . ." Perhaps my friends fundamentally honor my judicial
manner even as they might daily ridicule it, because any
roaming band of imaginary brothers wants its voice of restraint even as its members flee from real fathers in order to
roam without restraints.

My role becomes a triumph and a liability, the one deepen-
ing my capacity to endure the other. I become a listener, an
adviser, a judge, a defender of our public truth to our parents, to adults, to cops, and enough of a willing fighter under
provocation to earn my authority.

Through these adolescent years, the fifteen or so of us who
are central to this gang grow from each other and into each
other. We are of bone and blood together, and if not unique

to Brooklyn at that time, or even to other American cities, we
are, without being aware of it, unique to the world. A Jewish
gang roaming a Jewish neighborhood, possessing it for each
other in defiance of all others, the tribe in its own territory.
In my more stable adolescence, I am fattening up on all that
was left out of my boyhood. Meanwhile, in Europe, those
people from whom our parents came are, in those same
years, being slaughtered daily by the thousands.

In the rooms above a store, as I grow older and spend more
time in the kitchen in the evenings perfunctorily mastering
college homework and waiting to be drafted, there is always
the radio. Ceaselessly my father listens to the news. For him
the name of Hitler becomes the house obscenity as well as
the slop-jar depository for all that has been shit and outrage
in his own life. Conversely, he celebrates the Russians (Soviet
style), from whose military draft he fled Warsaw in 1913 and
came to America. He wants to argue politics with me, but I
back off. To his dismay, I am preoccupied with ball games
and girls, and the reading that I enjoy comes from novels and
poems. And I suspect my father's monologues that begin as
diatribes against capitalism (which I cruelly discount as the
sour grapes of a loser) and end with nostalgic remembrances
in praise of European culture. I distrust what I understand
others to mean by culture, for I have already begun to believe that on the grand scale it goes to bed with the barbari-
ans. In a freshman course in the classics, I turn blind to the
beauties of Greek architecture as soon as I learn that slaves
were used to build the great holy temples. And the history
I am made to read I fail to understand as anything more than
a compilation of dates recording the murders that led to the
treaties that led to the murders. I am as full of outrage as
anyone else at social injustice, but I have limited appreciation
for social solutions. Almost a junior in college when I am

eighteen, I am a political imbecile. It comes hard to me at Brooklyn College to find differences among the Trotskyites, who spit on the Stalinists, the Stalinists who curse the socialists, and the autocratic college president who shits on all of them. I am already on that track where I find it difficult to separate the thing that's said from the person who says it when I know the person and am dubious about the thing.

I know my friends concretely. I have never seen a Nazi. At the age of eighteen my ability to put my body where the commitment is is confined to the actual community in which I live. As I travel on the familiar subway to my army physical in Manhattan—balancing a fantasy of heroism and a dimly felt sense of cause against the more vivid sense of the lonely and foreign life I would embark on to achieve that heroism and serve that cause—I am clear about only one desire, itself a fantasy: if most, or half, or even a third, or a few of my friends could come with me and serve at my side, I could become a giant of a world citizen, fighting anywhere with them against any form of tyranny over the mind of man. Hell, with my friends there I might even on some occasion fight on the wrong side.

At Grand Central Palace I am rejected for military service: bad vision, punctured eardrums, a trick knee. I return that day to a Hitler-hating father who embraces me with congratulations, and a mother who, adoring F.D.R., cries in relief. They are also concrete. I am released back into my daily world for the year and a half that is left to the war. When some of my friends in that stretch of time begin to depart for the service, I am in my junior year at college, majoring in English and playing football on a team of 4-F's and those not yet old enough to be drafted. I am, as well, released from the most significant male experience of my generation.

Because of this enormous omission, I have little right to

respond, so many years later, to the married graduate student whose commitments in his maturity are so much more informed by principle and honor than were mine in my immaturity. And he is being asked to take up arms in a war where the wrong and the barbarism is on our side. I cannot even congratulate him on his principles or his commitments until I am ready, with him, to leave the country or go to jail. And if I am not ready to do that, given again the tyranny of my new circumstances, my own family now, then what can *I* teach *him* when I teach?

I stood on the fringe of a crowd of about two thousand at yet another noontime crisis rally on the campus in November. Not far from me, one of the most articulate of the black student leaders, tall, husky, in his middle twenties, suddenly broke from the crowd and rushed toward an isolated white student who was holding a few books. There was a brief exchange of words I couldn't hear. The white student was much shorter, younger. Suddenly the Black jabbed with his left, but with an open hand, as though for the moment it was still honor and not yet rage. It was a hard and stinging blow. It caught the white off balance and he toppled to the grass. His books scattered. He started to rise, and the Black stood over him, his right arm waiting, fisted, but his eyes darting to take in those who were beginning to look. Perhaps he too was looking for some way out of it. The white student, rising and scrambling backward at the same time, held a hand in front of his face to ward off another blow. He pleaded in a voice cracking with fear and humiliation. "I'm on *your* side. What are you hitting *me* for? I'm on *your* side." For a second the Black looked puzzled, his right arm still raised and his fist clenched. I trembled as I watched. I shared the humiliation of the one who'd been hit, and anxiety dried my mouth in anticipation of what my own role might have to be. I couldn't stand there and continue to watch. Neither could I turn my back.

At forty-three, I was no longer a fighter, but I felt the ordinary obligation to break it up. When the black student left, I breathed with relief.

For the next few weeks, until the Christmas recess, the noon rallies were daily confrontations between thousands of aroused students and hundreds of unpredictable police who had the lawful power to maim and kill. I kept telling myself to stop watching it on television's evening news and hiding from it on the campus itself. I had to get further away from it, or go more deeply into it, this brutal, senseless, daily violence. On television it had the terrible fascination of a battle ground on a territory where you worked and could identify, not only the buildings, but the very offices, and occasionally, the faces in the mob. On the campus itself, it was a horror I couldn't watch. It could not have been an accident that for all I saw on television, and in the photos of the newspapers, and heard from stories no one could stop telling, I never saw, on the campus itself, even one of the actual bloody beatings. I didn't even see the blood. On a number of occasions a squad of police rushed right by me, their clubs ready, but the selected victim was so quickly surrounded, I couldn't see what was being done to him. And I moved away. I wouldn't wait to see. And in all those days, I kept telling myself there was something I had to do. I had to go further away or deeper in —but what was deeper in? Could I rescue anyone or anything by offering my head to a club, getting arrested? And what was further out? Could I sit in my office and pretend it wasn't there? Could I look down on it from windows? What was the real nature, anyway, of this heart-eating debate with myself? Was I holding out for the use of at least my own reason, around which I had organized my adult life, or by now had the use of all that reason argued violence not only out of my mind, but out of my nature as well?

I am fourteen and in a neighborhood grade school gym open for the summer. I quarrel with another boy whose hair is very dark and who is stripped to the waist and sweating. He's Italian. It's the usual kid argument: threats, some curses, stopping before the fighting—both still able to walk out of it and still able to believe the other was chicken. Then, quickly, even before I can remove the glasses I am wearing, he charges, head down, arms flailing, his head grinding against my chest. I hang my left arm around the back of his neck, and with my eyes to the ceiling I swing again and again at a face I can't see. The flesh I hit is no harder than a melon. I get tired and stop. He stumbles away. His arms are already at his side, and he has already quit. His face is covered with the blood that pours from his nose. For the first time, I am terrified. If he raises his arms to fight again, I might run. But he doesn't know that; he has already quit. That night, in bed, I keep telling myself: "I made him bleed. I hit him and hit him, and he was all full of blood." I am only fourteen and I feel sweet with pride and immediacy. The fist I keep making is something to contemplate in the dark, as if it weren't the hand closed, but an object felt in the hand. I know the ecstasy that lives inside the lunacy of violence.

Then I am a senior at Brooklyn College five years later; I am captain of the football team and majoring in English—an all-American youth, a jock. I call the plays in the huddle, and the middle-aged man I have become in the life I now lead hears with a sometimes envious astonishment that nineteen-year-old ghost clapping his hands in the ritual of breaking the huddle, snarling: "Hit the bastards! Kill 'em!" I play in the confusion of the vague forms my bad eyes perceive, and I enjoy most what comes up closest: the initial spring through a hole in the line and the first cut past it; or, on defense, backing the line, and getting that angle on the runner when his direction is lateral and yours is forward, and he is running out of his room before he can make his cut. He can outweigh you by fifty pounds and be twice as fast, but when you own that angle, you can cut him off his feet as cleanly and emphatically as a single bullet can fell a horse.

Football is a remarkable American violence. You can't play it well without physical rage, nor can you play it well without removing most of the emotion from the rage. The rules and conditions provide for the restraint as well as the recklessness, and the tension between the two necessities makes even some of the pros tremble on the sidelines before the game. Out on the field, the game itself is even rougher than it looks to the viewer in the stands, but until the player is really busted up, he makes much less of the total violence than the witness does.

The student was in my office because he had made a scene in my class, objecting to the assignment of a term paper. He had said it was a useless exercise, boring for him to write, and all the more boring for me because I had to read not only his paper, but those of the others in the class, and perhaps of other classes as well. He didn't come to the office to apologize, but to admit rather angrily that he hadn't been able to establish his point in class. I had answered him by delivering a sermon on the occasion, and he wasn't about to, because he wasn't able to, compete with me when I occupied the academic pulpit with all its invested authority at the front of the room.

He was in his early twenties and married and having a hard

time in his marriage. His hair was long, but kinky; it grew out of his head like a huge Brillo ball. He was from the Bronx, and we were able, on one level, to make immediate provincial connections. He had run with a tough gang that had got him into things I had never even come to glimpse in what I still thought of as my own tough adolescence: knives, guns, drugs. He was one of the brighter students in the class, as well as a writer of some talent. He knew himself and his own implications with painful perception, and out of that knowledge he came quickly to some part of the center of any fiction we read. He used that as his complaint about term paper assignments. "I can say what I know in ten sentences. The rest is academic bullshit." In my office he mentioned that he had come to San Francisco State after starting and quitting at two other colleges because he had read an article I'd written about State. But since his coming, there had been nothing but disappointment, the same old crud. Because my article had conveyed the impression of a liberal college open even to an excess of possibility and experiment, the implication was clear. Not only had I misrepresented, I was part of the crud.

"Look," he argued, "I've gotten papers back here last semester with A's on all of them. You ought to read the comments. They knock me out. I'll bring you the papers. You read the paper, and then read the prof's comment. He tells me, 'brilliant insights,' 'fine mind,' 'an excellent sense of the subject.' I keep taking them out of the desk and looking at the comments, and I can't stop laughing. The papers are just full of bullshit. Just putting the garbage back in the can, that's all it is. I'm not playing that game any more. Not with you. These term papers are not relevant to my life or yours. I have a stake in your judgment about it. I expect you to think I'm right."

I told him to do the paper. I said that if he could get an A from me and laugh at it, then we had something to talk about. Right now, before the fact of the paper, all I could see was more self-indulgence in the place of an argument. "As though you were the first of students," I said, continuing the sermon of the class, "in the first generation of such students, to confront the limits of the possibilities of studying a subject like English in an academic place." In class I had said that the argument about term papers wasn't where the argument was. We had to talk about what we meant in coming together in the first place through course after course in a subject called "English." By it we mainly meant literature, by which we meant, discarding the assumption of remedial reading, that there was still something left for the teacher himself to accomplish. It was something more humanly rich than information alone, and yet more factual than mere insight. Relevance in such a subject only meant, as far as I could see, the teacher himself and the community he made in and through the class, and through the book and the author, a context within a context, where there was a mind in the passion, and passion in the mind. The teacher as well as the book had to come out whole. What else could "relevant" mean when one kind of teacher could make Beckett or Faulkner irrelevant, and another could make of medieval literature a drama in the streets or paradise in a meadow? But they were demanding the impossible if they for one minute believed that in a school of our size, in a department as large as ours, they weren't going to have their share of boring teachers. In which case, I said, and pointed toward the library, "Your total opportunity for that class is where the books are. As for the term papers, that's your opportunity to give me what's total in yourselves. And if it only comes to ten sentences, you better start worrying about the sum."

Good reasoning, resounding words. But for many days afterward, they were to linger in my mouth with an acid taste of fraud. The impassioned words were unanswerable for the very reason perhaps that they had not themselves answered some other question. That taste was there again during the talk in my office with the student who had started it all. He couldn't answer me, but neither had I answered him. It was not the kind of difference where words alone could do it. He wrote the paper, got a B, and dropped out of school. I haven't seen or heard from him since. He could have been a good student. In the most ideal way, he already was. But toward what end should he have remained in college with a major in English, having already decided he couldn't bear to go for an M.A. and Ph.D., with more classes and more papers, in order to teach and himself be, for all his life, a part of all *this?* When I asked him what he would do if he quit college, he shrugged. He wasn't too worried. He looked at me as though all *that* was exactly my hang-up. He was used to living poor. And Vietnam? He was already rejected. He had put on a great act before the psychiatrist.

"Yeah, I know," he said. "You have to be crazy in the first place to get away with that. But I am. I look at myself in the mirror in the morning, and I say, 'You're crazy.'" He took hold of his hair. "Anybody going out on the street looking like this has got to be crazy."

I am twenty when I graduate from Brooklyn College and look for a job. I am twenty-one when I enroll at Columbia for a master's. In the year between I work for five months as a copy boy—enough to know that newspapers are for me neither the way to earn a living nor to fulfill the grand and ignorant sense I have of the writing I want to do. I get the degree in two semesters—nine months. I write a two-hundred-page thesis, pass the written exams, work part-time in a settlement house, skip most of my classes, and graduate with honors. I meet none of my professors, I never consult my thesis director, and no one knows my name. From my professors at Columbia I learn mostly what should *not* be done in a classroom to prevent the dying of the spirit and the murder of the books and authors we are supposed to honor by our gathering.

At twenty-two I get married. We go to the University of Kansas, where my teaching begins. Two years later I am a part-time teacher at the University of Iowa and enrolled again as a graduate student in what will be a four-year grind for the Ph.D. In the middle of that time we return to New York one summer and I visit an old neighborhood playground. I see someone I know shooting baskets. I say to myself, "Jesus, he is still doing what I last saw him doing when he was eighteen." He stops long enough to ask me what I am doing and where I have been. And when I tell him I'm back at school, he says, "Jesus! You're still in school?" He rolls his eyes in pure wonder at the unimaginable mysteries I am trying to unravel. What could keep me in school past my middle twenties when he quit it all at sixteen? He knows I'm not going to be a physician.

I leave Kansas because I can't hope to remain there or go anywhere else on my terms without the Ph.D. I can gamble on the writing, but that's the bind I was trying to get out of in the first place. I can lead a decent and useful life in the teaching if I lose out on the writing, but as low man on the department ladder, I will always be in the same shape I am in at Kansas: sixty freshman themes a week that take me thirty hours to correct and are only the beginning of my responsibilities. It leaves me little time for writing. The means are defeating the ends, but there is no way of dodging the responsibilities or abandoning the ambition. I can't give up the security for the gamble of the writing and live poor, because as a kid I *did* live poor and saw it crush my parents. I need the security in order to endure the postponement of rewards. A man of a temperament other than mine might worry more that he could in this fashion take his postponements to his grave, but I am still much too young and healthy to be impressed by coffin-thoughts. I choose, then, to toss a variety of necessities through the air around my life.

At Iowa the juggling lasts four years. I now have three degrees, have spent nine years for them on three different campuses, have attended more than seventy classes, have had at least forty different professors, in whose classes I wrote term papers and took exams to numbers beyond my memory. For a kid who started out with school as a place for renewed shocks every time my family moved, I ended by taking the bitch to bed. But as a student, it was never a very hot affair. Of all those professors, I can count on one hand the number who moved my life by altering even slightly my sense of the subject they taught, or of the world I knew or imagined, or of myself. I can count on two hands the classrooms that didn't finally bore me. Wherever the fault lies, in me, or the professors, or beyond us, I do know this: given the subjects that meant anything to me, in four years of being left to myself, I could have read more and learned more than in those nine years of prescribed doses. Left to myself, I might even have joyfully pursued my own discoveries in the personal sequence in which they are most meaningfully made. But I would have been a bum also—a learned man without learned degrees signed by college presidents and boards of trustees.

The marvel is that I know all that through most of these nine years. Often I think of quitting along the way, especially during the Ph.D., but my capacity to endure the inherited conventions is remarkable. I tell myself that I am ultimately doing it for myself. Finally the messy table will be swept clean of *their* requirements, and I'll get at my own food. It never occurs to me to organize or participate in a revolt against the system itself. Even if there had been a style for it, I should have declined. Not because I lack the ego for revolt, but because I have too much. There are so many others who find the system suitable. The discontent, I reassure myself, is my measure of uniqueness against what is common in this or any other system. Moreover, serving ego, I always need to finish what I start. I won't have to believe later that I quit because I was incapable of finishing. Having won my credentials, I could then repudiate them.

Through these nine student years, then, I play the game by the rules of the game. The phrase, coming out of the school-yard, runs through my life, despite the fact that the arbitrariness of the rules never stops occurring to me. In adolescence I want to know why you can't run the bases the other way. Why did *they* make it counterclockwise when most of the imitating circles go the clock's way? But I never try it out the other way. It will cost me a turn at bat, and I'd just as soon not play as not bat. And there's the waste of disorder in inventing your own rules along the way. Beyond fatuous analogy, but still into my own life, the dilemma, of course, is ageless.

I walked through the corridors of the Administration Building at San Francisco State College late in the spring of 1968. Students, led by the SDS, were staging a mill-in. They were banging with fists and heels against the walls and locked office doors. At the first open office I saw a gang of shouting students seated at and standing before two desks. One of them, using the telephone, was in the swivel chair. Suddenly, he put his hand over the mouthpiece and commanded the others: "Quiet down. Everybody shut up! I have Paris on the line!"

I walked down the corridor to the office of an administrative aide I knew. He was in his chair against a wall, trying to appear calm but looking shot. He was surrounded by a group of students. They all turned to me when I entered. In a strained voice the administrative aide introduced me. "Let him come in. He's a good guy." He gave my name and department. I felt grim, but I laughed. Did he mean that if he hadn't interceded with praise they would have thrown me out? I explained to the woman nearest me, who was sitting on a corner of my friend's desk, that I was returning to a Humanities School meeting and wanted to report what was going on here. We had heard about the long-distance calls, and I mentioned the episode I had just witnessed. She thrust her face at me.

"Suppose I want to call my mother now and say hello? You're not going to stop me. What are you so uptight about long-distance calls for? Are they costing the state too much money? Do you know how much money it costs to drop a bomb on Vietnam?" She put her hand near the phone. "If I want to call my mother, I'll call my mother."

My impulse, suppressed, was to deliver a sermon on the spot. It would have mentioned reason, distinctions, conduct, methods, results. Later in the afternoon I saw Litwak, who was on leave but had returned for the day to take in our scene. He was surprised I took the phone calls so seriously. I was surprised he could so easily dismiss them. "It's not the real issue," he said. But my own sense of the reasonable locked like a clamp over the amusements of confrontation theater in my own backyard. I still believed in a campus dependent on rational persuasion.

In my senior year at Brooklyn College I am president of the Men's Athletic Association, and together with my friend, who is vice-president, serve on the Faculty-Student Committee of Athletics. The business that comes before us is routine: budget, schedules, complimentary tickets. But the year before we suffered a point-fixing basketball scandal, and now all routine matters are dealt with as if each decision bears the burden of the destiny of the college and the fate of higher education in America. At a meeting I am about to attend, we are to vote on a minor issue now dressed in magnitude. For the students and the athletes we've been elected to represent, it becomes vital to myself and my friend that the votes fall to us. He declares that if the vote goes 5–2 against us once more, he's going to rap one of those profs in the teeth and quit the committee. I try to calm him down.

"When we get to the meeting, you shut up. Let me do all the talking. I'll reason with them. I'll make them see it."

"The way you did last time when the vote was five to two? And the time before that? I'm getting sick of it. There's not even one faculty member on that committee who goes to any of our games. Why the hell should they even be voting?"

"Just let me do the talking, will you?"

I actually believe it. I believe in reason and my own power to make use of it. I save my anger for bad people acting malevolently, but these mild professors, with their own reasonable talk, are not what I mean by bad men. It will take me years and years to learn that bad men don't wear horns and good ones aren't lit with halos. I still have difficulty believing it today.

I think I am being eloquent at the meeting. I am calm, serious. I make careful distinctions; my voice resonates with moral fervor. I know they know I major in English and not phys. ed., and if they haven't seen me play football they have all read a poem of mine in the college literary magazine. I

tell myself it has a cash value. I sense the impression I make
on them as I talk. They look at each other from time to time
and nod their heads in approval. Just before the voting, the
dean of students appears as a guest and speaks for a moment
on the other side of the question. And then the president of
the college appears. He says nothing on the question but
merely greets the chairman of the committee—very jovial
this greeting. Then he sits down to await the vote. It's again
5–2.

The Main Auditorium of San Francisco State College in the
week of November 19, 1968, was continously packed with
faculty and students attending the "educational" convocation to discuss the fifteen nonnegotiable demands of the BSU
and TWLF. On stage were student leaders of those organizations, as well as representatives of the administration and
faculty. Time and again the students made it plain that the
convocation was not to be misunderstood as negotiating ses-
sions. Their demands were nonnegotiable. They had acquiesced to the suggestion of the convocation only for the
purpose of educating the college, and the community generally, about the racist nature of our institution and about the
revolutionary meaning of relevance in higher education.
Time and again we were told by one student leader or another that this college hereafter would never be the same.
Again and again we were told of the life in the ghettos in San
Francisco, not only Fillmore and Hunter's Point, but Chinatown and the Spanish-speaking Mission district. Occasionally
a black or Third World member of the college administration
participated on the side of the students. Dr. Juan Martinez,
whose reappointment to the History Department in the previous semester was an issue in the spring demonstrations,
reminded us that California itself was an occupied territory,

seized from his Mexican ancestors. Dr. Joseph White, the
new dean of undergraduate studies, who bore a slight resem-
blance to James Baldwin, informed us that he himself had
been an undergraduate student at this college, and that we
were now, all of us at the convocation, getting more of an
education in a couple of days than he had ever gotten in all
his years here.

It was an occasion. I was moved by all of it. I did not
entirely believe any of it.

"You are either a part of the problem or a part of the
solution," Eldridge Cleaver had admonished the few thousand of us who, a few weeks before the convocation, had
gathered to hear him on the speaker's platform before the
open quad in the center of the campus, where, a month later,
the bloody and unpredictable confrontations with police
would become a daily noontime exercise. Cleaver moved
most of us as he played on all the public-speaking keys of
stirring rhetoric, sober responsibility, obscene insult, satani-
cally Biblical anecdote, and badgering humor. I was not altogether persuaded of anything. A harangue and a mob come
finally into their own endangering limitations. It was not my
sense of education, or even greatly clarifying. "What if," I
asked Cleaver through myself, "what if *your* solution is a part
of the problem?"

Words. Words and more words. More reservations and
more distinctions. We were only a month away from violence
and chaos.

I return briefly to New York in mid April of 1969 to attend
to a family emergency. It is now several days since the last
of the police have left their daily, uninterrupted occupation
of the campus that began an incredible five months before,
in November. My first evening in New York is free, and I go

with the friends who meet me at the airport—a psychiatrist and his wife—to the tail end of a dinner party in Brooklyn Heights, a prior obligation they couldn't cancel. There are other physicians present, as well as an aide to Mayor Lindsay, and the conversation is predominantly about community health programs and problems. By community they mean ghetto, and Brownsville is the ghetto they most often refer to. It should be of special interest to me. Brownsville takes me back almost to my own beginnings; and the so-recent experience at San Francisco State was most immediately precipitated by racial issues. But these two beginnings span some thirty-five years of my life, and in the past six months I have listened to and talked of almost nothing else. And now again, this evening, among strangers, three thousand miles from home and not exactly sure any more which side of the continent is home for me, over the brandy and the Cointreau and the crème de menthe, the familiar words lose their meaning for me. I've heard them too often. They drop out of their sentences because there is no longer any edge to such worn-out words to lock them into contexts: "society," "priorities," "leadership," "budget," "group dynamics." What most oppresses me is how essentially good these people are, and how they work and hope for the accomplishment of a decent thing. But the rent for this house, I am told, is six hundred dollars a month, and the self-conscious old street on which it stands looks as if it were restored as a setting for *The Barretts of Wimpole Street.* The difference between the words that are used here to deal with the ghetto and the ghetto words as they are lived by those who cannot leave its streets or improve them is the leap you make between saying "society," on the one hand, and "motherfucker," on the other.

My friend's wife, sensitive to my strangeness there, my silence, my obvious weariness, tries to bring me into the conversation. She mentions to those nearest her that I teach at San Francisco State. It raises eyebrows and produces questions, but of a kind in which I sense the interest as a momentary curiosity about a remotely provincial event. But I cannot either fully or concisely answer the questions even if the interest might be total. The past six months have been too complicated for conciseness. And for the full, even if uncertain, answers, there is nothing that will do short of the unraveling of the threads of my own life as well as the sequences of our provincially public events at the college.

Three days later I am driving a car in that Brownsville ghetto. I pass the intersection of Saratoga and Bergen, where my father, in the depths of the Depression, had opened another grocery store. Within a year it had failed again and we moved again. He sits beside me now in the car and remembers nothing of this. He is in his late seventies, a widower for fifteen years, and now senile. Such memory as he has left is most often hooked on Europe. Over and over again he repeats the tale of how he crossed the border from Poland into Germany in order to come to America and escape the Russian draft. He remarks occasionally, in response to what he sees out the window, that this neighborhood is full of Blacks. "Are we still in Brooklyn?" he asks. I drive on Bergen Street past that row of desolate tenements in one of which there are the rooms where I had lived. If it was a slum thirty-five years ago, what can it be called now? If so many years ago it was already an outrage to acquire income through the rental of such rooms, what is it to be called today when the kids who inhabit such rooms share the advantages of television to remind them through hours of canned domestic comedy and detective drama that their own world is truly unique? In the world of that TV screen, which must be real because it is being watched all through the country, there are no rats, there are no black criminals, there are no busted whiskey bottles or syringe vials. There aren't even any classrooms where the teacher can call it a good professional day at four when she is home safe, call it good not for what was learned or taught but because she is, finally, home and safe.

I drive another block and come to Dean Street. I have remembered the name all these years but have not recalled it as the particular street where I visited one day after school in the cellar under the house, where my black classmate lived and his father was so sullen and silent. I have to stop the car at a red light, and a group of black men in their twenties cross the street before me. One of them glances at us. My father is too imprisoned by his stupefaction to witness what he sees, but the hatred in that black man's quick look is driven through my skull. There are no distinctions to be made here. Whatever credentials I carry, whatever history I have accumulated, whatever the degrees after my name, or books I have written and hope to write, the lectures delivered, the papers graded, the committees served on, the complaints and confessions listened to, the advice offered, whatever in my presumption I have imagined I have taught through so many countless authors and books and poems that are themselves testaments against inhumanity and celebrations of the imagination's passion for beauty, whatever I have learned in the past six months about my own nature, my own way of life, and this very intersection of this Brooklyn ghetto, now three thousand miles from my home but where I once lived and played, waiting even then, though I didn't know it, to get out of it—none of that can possibly be the beginning of being enough to arrest or alter the look of that black man glancing at me as he crosses the street, the look saying it as completely as the word. Motherfucker! And in the word, and in the look, is the beginning of the war waiting for us all.

Guiltless or guilty, we are all entangled.

It will be, finally, as it finally was at San Francisco State, something larger than its own immediate racial origins. For they are enough, the racial origins, as fact and as metaphor, to split us so wide that all other issues, invented and real, small and great, can come alive inside the breach.

3 · San Francisco State College: the background

HERBERT WILNER

It's a streetcar college of ninety-four acres in the southwestern corner of San Francisco, about a mile from the Pacific. In September 1967, there were about fifteen buildings, most of them long, low, rectangular, banded with windows and painted in shades of institutional beige. The walks were narrow, the landscaping tidy, and here and there a single cypress or a cluster of pines survived the bulldozing that had cleared the way for the buildings. Everything bore the look of having arrived in cartons marked "instant campus," giving off the air—not altogether unpleasant, rather banal—like so much else that's new in California, of being temporary, of the cartons being kept ready for a return shipment to the maker in case the college didn't work, or the State of California no longer wanted it.

It *was* an instant campus. The college occupied its present site in the early fifties when it left the few downtown buildings that had housed it as a small liberal arts college recently transformed from a teachers' college. When I first came to S.F. State in 1957, there were eight thousand students and more than four hundred faculty, and the place, even then, was in a clerical uproar. They fully expected ten thousand students by 1960! By 1967 there were over eighteen thousand students and around one thousand faculty. It was a bewildering growth, and for these years of adolescence it compelled unremitting self-examinations. Who are we?

Where are we going? Why? The questions were fed into the everlasting committees also compelled by the growth—and such answers as were returned to the faculty were debated until the answers and the debates were no longer applicable because another dramatic change had taken place in size, in budget, in the membership of the committee, in the administration, in the composition of the student body or the faculty. Or there had been, in the meantime, directives from the agencies upstairs, telling the adolescent college what it really had to do and what it really had to be.

Two of these agencies for all the state colleges were the offices of the chancellor, occupied by Glenn S. Dumke and the board of trustees. The agencies were created in the early sixties by a drawing-board scheme called the Master Plan for Higher Education. The plan, incorporated into the State Code, was to regulate all the growing state colleges in a structure that was aware of, parallel to, but apart from the University of California system. In other words, the state colleges, with lower admission standards, would provide for more students but be second best in quality and resources. Two of the effects of this plan on faculty and students at S.F. State were a daily mountain of paper reports and requirements, and with awesome Berkeley across the bay, a self-consciousness about an unalterable second place that produced, at S.F. State, scholarly imitations or offbeat originals.

The offbeat, at first, was congenial to the spirit of the college. In the late fifties, for instance, the work of the Poetry Center and the Creative Writing Program was already nationally known. Through the sixties they helped to attract and build an impressive English Department that balanced out between the offbeat and the more orthodox. The greatest lure, of course, in the building of the entire faculty and its better-than-average departments for a state college was San

Francisco itself. The S F. State prof was almost insolent in his smugness of place. He certainly believed he was living in the best community in California. He might have believed it was the preferred place in the country. Identification with the college took on the same pride of place that went with San Francisco itself, and I knew of colleagues who turned down offers from major universities in other states that improved on salaries, working conditions, and prestige, in order not to give up San Francisco. The pride contributed a feisty quality to the faculty. They would set aside differences and summon this spirit to take on together the authorities of the chancellor and the trustees, and to support, or pretend to support, an open attitude toward curriculum and experiment.

The students who kept swelling the college were hard to classify, though by 1967, the outsider, especially the one who lived in the Bay Area, would have inclined to make him typical: bearded, beaded, barefoot, high on pot or stoned on acid, hitching rides between Haight-Ashbury and the college, at least friendly to the SDS, envious of and in love with Blacks. But there was no typical S.F. State student, even then. In my decade at the college, the classroom had always been an event in the unpredictable. If the majority of students were older and working part-time or full-time, there was shared among them only the unpredictability of their great differences. Some were twenty-five, some were thirty-five or older. Few of them had been raised in San Francisco. Some felt an identification with the college; some held no more feelings for it than they did for the Motor Vehicle Bureau. It was a place to get a goal accomplished—gather what credentials you were after, and then get off the license lines. If there were some students who would have liked on particular days to linger on the campus, there was no way. Those who had sent the college in its cartons had forgotten a student union.

It was through the students that the college became, for me, such a life-touched place. Perhaps this quality was personally exaggerated through the greater intimacies of a creative writing program, but I imagined it was generally so elsewhere in the college. Academic intentions weren't undermined, but they were certainly startled by my students: women who were raising or had raised their children; a woman who had built an isolated ranch house with her own hands; a thirty-five-year-old ex-carpenter who was thinking of divorcing his wife because his new life as a student was such an intellectual awakening and she didn't and wouldn't read; a retired rear admiral who'd been through most of the battles of the Pacific and Korean War; a younger man who defied the Navy and the government by navigating a small crew on a sailboat into atomic test waters in the Pacific; a red-faced ex-alcoholic with arteries throbbing in his neck like garden hoses—and all of them, through the years, mixed together in the classrooms, not only with each other, but with students of the ordinary ages, between eighteen and twenty-two, who looked like babies.

There were times when I wished myself free of the burden of them all. It was not my subject and the teaching of it that so often drained me. It was the pressure of needing to do right by these so variously endowed people, as people and not as students.

In the middle sixties a new kind of student did indeed come to the college in great numbers from the Haight-Ashbury, but only after they had come to the Haight-Ashbury from everywhere, in the thousands. They complicated the already complex unpredictability. Most of the hippies were too much into their own styles to organize or individually protest whatever they thought were the lunacies of the college as an academic establishment. But there was inevitable interchange between them and the reborn campus activists, and the relationships were intensified by the role San Francisco was playing as a national center for the gathering of dissidence against the American contradictions. Their ways and voices reached all the students, and S.F. State acted out, in miniature, a new kind of melting pot. Even before the college came to ultimate crisis, the numbers game was already being played in the continued self-examinations that were now more strained, conducted in louder voices. Who are our students who speak for the students? And all over again: Who are we educating for what?

The faculty itself was too varied to offer coherent guidance. The adolescent college was too young and too recently big to have any traditions to pull down and build from, or with which to bull its way through the new questions. The college had a tradition of experimentalism, if one could call it that, but who knew who and what to experiment for? There had been an emphatic tradition of liberalism in the faculty, but who knew what that would mean in a crisis, or on what extreme side of a crisis, the right or the left, the liberal would find his particular devil? There were, for example, forty-year-old profs who were not unsympathetic to the new student forces on the campus, who came to meetings with a plan tucked in their pockets for what they thought was a dramatic revision of curriculum, of student affairs, of whatever, only to be addressed at the meeting by a much younger colleague, newly arrived—perhaps with his Ph.D. just earned at Berkeley through the years leading up to the Free Speech Movement riots in 1965—who heard the plan out and then shook his head in scorn or pity or genuine despair and said, "You really don't know where it's at. You don't know what kind of fascist you really are."

A few students, tired of all this and out of a deliberate platform of student initiative, officers in the student government and skilled at organizing the improvised, in 1965 began something called the Experimental College. Using the few crowded huts housing student activity offices, they offered courses unavailable in the college curriculum. There was no credit for the students, no pay for the teachers. It was bulletin-board operation: anyone who felt himself qualified could announce his course; anyone interested could take it. The avowed intention of the student organizers was to expand the intellectual offerings of the college by avoiding that impenetrable graveyard of the system where all possibilities died in dead committees. The impact was immense.

Enrollments were high. The college took notice. The administration paid attention. Educators everywhere in the country watched. Magazines wrote. John Summerskill, the college's newly-appointed president, young, flexible, a former Cornell administrator, appointed a committee to look into the possibility of the college founding a formal School of Experimental Studies, or something like that. In the meantime, the student improvisation got some needed money from the student government (Associated Students), and for one semester, hired Paul Goodman as a free-floating counselor and teacher, available to the college at large, and hired LeRoi Jones in the same role the following semester. Some faculty volunteered their teaching services, and some departments arranged for the sponsorship of courses for credit.

But confusion prevailed. The conditions which produced the Experimental College made it succeed, and the success, in those conditions, chewed it up. Hippies taught and entered the courses in such numbers that academic possibilities got submerged in concoctions that were all the more idiotic because they were serious, even solemn, like a "course" in nonverbal deep meditation. And there were factional political fights among the students for their share of the money and the limited space. There was the perverse problem of keeping bureaucracy and the college out and improvisation in, when the structure of the free model had already grown so large so fast. There were even rumors that student political organizations were moving in with muscle.

By September 1967, then, S.F. State College was big, prideful, confused, mixed, noisy, busy, dizzy, humanly warm-blooded, and still, despite it all, optimistic, even aggressively so. If some of the optimism was the result of mistaking noise for excitement, and excitement for activity, and activity for action, the delusion itself could keep it going for years and years, the college perhaps finding out as it went along that its delusion was its own particular form of life, and that life had a prominent contribution to make in a world of colleges not living that way.

It wasn't to be. There was the racial factor.

The percentage of "minority" students at S.F. State didn't correspond to the population figures of San Francisco. This was significantly true for students from Spanish-speaking homes and for Blacks. In fact, in the ten-year period ending in September 1967, the number of black students at the college had decreased in proportion to the college's total student enrollment.

Among the new political organizations formed on the campus in the middle sixties was the Black Students Union. Their leaders argued the racist character of the college. Raising academic standards for admission in the past decade had not allowed for the needs of capable black students whose on-paper qualifications had been spoiled in a racist society through its racist system of public education.

The literal facts of the argument were incontrovertible. No black student making the argument could be concerned with any other aspect of the college's character, past or present—

except, perhaps, for the college's prideful awareness of trying for relevance of proclaiming for the academic traffic between community and campus. In that context the black student could speak of the ghettos of the Fillmore district and Hunter's Point. The rest of us would then know which people he had in mind when he said education for the people, or power to the people. Neither did we miss the fact—in the relatedness of campus and community—that the national headquarters of the Black Panthers was across the bay, in Oakland, a thirty-minute ride from the college.

4 · opening battles

HERBERT WILNER

I never paid much attention to the racial distribution of the student body. "There are a lot of Orientals around," I might have said to any inquiring outsider, and he would probably have nodded, thinking of Chinatown. I didn't count the number of black students at San Francisco State. I had never seen a large number of them on any campus. If I'd been asked why this was so, my answers would have been commonplace, and so, too, my suggestions for correcting the injustice. Start at the beginning, I would have said. Change the grade schools and the high schools, change the country, change the heart.

Actually, I imagined I saw more black students at S.F. State than I might have expected, and their numbers seemed to be increasing through the years. It was an impression I didn't bother to correct by analyzing proportional statistics, or by allowing for the inclination of black students to sit together in the cafeteria or move across the campus in groups. Most important, the college appeared to be quiet on the racial issue, and quiet meant good. If I heard something about squabbles among black and white students over funds from the large treasury of the Associated Students, what I heard wasn't loud. Discussions and arguments about something called Black Studies were of little importance to me. Somewhere on campus it would get settled.

My own recognition of the real conflicts about the issues of race and higher education on our campus took place on November 6, 1967. On that day, fourteen black students, some of them leaders of the Black Students Union, entered the offices of the college newspaper in the Humanities Building. A little while later, they left. The place was a shambles.

Papers were strewn, chairs overturned, desks out of place, typewriters on the floor. The student editor had been beaten and hospitalized. A part-time teacher of journalism had a broken finger. All the staff members present at the time were white, and most of them felt terrorized. One of them, however, a photographer with a camera handy, snapped a role of pictures during the melee. Some of them were printed the next day in local newspapers, and then nationally. All the pictures were submitted to President Summerskill with corroborating identifications and individual accounts by the *Gater* staff. The black students involved offered no alternative version of what had happened. They were in hiding, following charges from the district attorney's office of a double felony—assault, and conspiracy to commit assault. Summerskill promptly suspended the black students. He protected their rights to due process on the campus by making their suspensions temporary, pending their appearance before a college disciplinary committee.

In a few days the black students, surrendering, were advised by their lawyers not to appear before the college disciplinary committee. The process could place them in double jeopardy. If the committee found against them, what chance would they have in court? So the college committee proceeded without their testimony and Summerskill acted upon its recommendation. Two of the students were suspended for a year, two for the semester; the others received probation and reprimand.

A curious legal nicety in campus affairs presented itself in the person of one of the suspended, a graduate student in English named George Murray, who was also a teacher in the freshman composition program. Summerskill, again mindful of due process, sent a memorandum to the English Department suggesting that the suspension of Murray come not from his office but the department. The English Department demurred, claiming its committees were not constituted to assure due process, but were guided by Murray's work as a teacher in the classroom—and all reports of that work were good. So Murray, suspended as a student, continued as a teacher. The newspapers made much of it, causing a public bewilderment that would change to anger in the following fall, when Murray, still teaching, had achieved the reputation of a Rap Brown of the Bay Area.

A civil verdict on the accused students did not take place until six months later, in April 1968. The case never went to jury trial. The lawyers for the students were able to establish at hearings that there had been no conspiracy to commit assault. The black students had intended to complain about what they called racist reporting. The editor kept them waiting a long time, invited a few of them into his inner office, kept them waiting again while he continued a phone call, and—when he was yelled at by one of the Blacks—responded with a racial slur. He got decked. The general fracas started when the Blacks, trying to leave the office, were denounced by the outraged teacher of journalism. The serious felony charges were dropped. The students pleaded guilty to the charge of misdemeanor, and the sentences were all probationary.

At the time of the event, only a handful of faculty members, trusted by the BSU, knew the above version. This inside information did not come out until six months later. To this day it would be fair to guess the majority of the faculty still doesn't know it at all. I know it now only because I've since met the lawyer for the students, and he told it to me one year after the hearing. The involved black students had simply chosen not to speak until the hearing, reminding us bitterly, in the meantime, that the facts were not all known.

A few days after the suspensions were announced, in November, a petition circulated in the English Department asking that the suspensions be lifted. I refused to sign. I was adamant about it. How could you guarantee due process to those who refused it? Double jeopardy was double-talk to me. If the case for the involved black students was unambiguously on their side, were they so committed to the beauty and purity of the principles of law that they wouldn't give their version of the story in a dozen different places, no less two, in order to show immediately the injustice of Summerskill's temporary suspensions? And all those photographs. You were blind if you didn't see a fistfight and a ransacked office in them. And there was nothing in my experience or my imagination to make me believe that any white person in the office could have swung first or made a racially insulting remark. It had nothing to do with my faith in the enlightened intelligence or civil decency of the newspaper staff. I simply assumed you don't swing at or say "nigger" to any one of fourteen black men who have come to your office for a redress of grievances on the issue of race.

And if someone had said to me, "You're a racist—you really think in the racist mold and don't even know it," then I would have said to him, "What the hell are you, then? If fourteen white jocks had come into that office and left us with the photographs and no willingness to correct it, you wouldn't now be circulating petitions—and you know it." But one month later, I was to stand up in a meeting of the Academic Senate after a manipulating and somewhat nasty speech there by James Garrett, then president of the BSU and one of those involved in the *Gater* incident, and make a plea on behalf of the suspended students. I would also appeal to Garrett and the

few other Blacks who were there to help us all find some
common ground for reconciliation on the campus.

In that intervening month, the BSU had built the *Gater*
incident into a major cause. The outcry against the suspensions was just the cutting edge for opening the whole argument for the increased admissions of black students and the
establishment of a Department of Black Studies. Rallies and
demonstrations began on campus, to which white student
political organizations added bulk and rhetoric. The SDS was
there, and the PLP, and an improvised outfit called MAPS—
Movement Against Political Suspensions.

And then one of the rallies erupted. Black student leaders
reached into their ghettos. Mothers came with children.
Adolescents and young men came. They raced through the
Administration Building, finding small targets for their rage:
wastebaskets to overturn, doors to pound on, walls to scratch.
Then the crowd spilled out to the open quad. The older
non-students took over. There were some blows. A window
of The Bookstore was smashed. Someone started a fire in The
Bookstore, but it was quickly extinguished. Some faculty
members, most of them known to the BSU, tried to restore
calm. One of them, a friend of mine, told me afterward that
a black youth in African dress, who was not a student of the
college, ran across the grass with a spear at his shoulder. My
friend ran after him, appealing to him. The youth finally
stopped, turned, stared. Then he raised the point of the spear
to my friend's throat.

"You don't mean a spear," I interrupted. "I heard some of
them carried umbrellas. They threatened people with the
points of the umbrellas, not a spear—"

"I mean a spear."

"You mean like a javelin?"

"Man, I mean a spear with a blade on the end of it."

Another colleague, a man who was then the director of the freshman English program and who had strongly recommended the initial appointment of George Murray to the staff, had been at my friend's side. He tried to offer "brother" credentials to the wild youth, and also the credentials of my friend, who was dean of undergraduate studies and working for a more open and relevant curriculum. He had worked with BSU leaders. The youth grew more frenzied with every pleading word. Finally a member of the BSU appeared. The spear-carrier turned to him. He indicated the freshman English director with a gesture of his head: "Get this white motherfucker to shut up!" he cried. The BSU member pacified him, and the professors stole off.

I listened to the story, and to others, and asked myself: What was going on? Where did it so suddenly come from? Why hadn't I been prepared for it? Instead of answers, my head filled with steaming images: Blacks, Africans, spears, dark marauders, jungle action.

We started immediately after the explosive rally to hold emergency meetings of the faculty. An immediate issue was to rescue President Summerskill. The trustees were ready to fire him. Why hadn't he called the police? His answer was simple and persuasive and received the unanimous support of the faculty. It was the last time we would be unanimous about anything, and it was perhaps the last time that a college president's answer to such a question would suffice. Police had told Summerskill not to call the police. Intelligence officers on campus believed the eruption was quickly losing the energy that squads of police could only refuel. The trustees had to acquiesce.

As I was leaving the Main Auditorium at the end of one of the faculty meetings, I saw a few black students at the doors. They leaned against the wall, arms folded over chests, and they stared at us. I glanced at them and kept walking. Their expressions were sullen, angry, but their posture, and the picture they made—I remember the picture and have long since forgotten everything that was said at the meeting—was of people who'd been transformed by language into objects. For the more than five hundred of us who had met inside the closed doors, black students had been our texts for discussion, analysis, speculation, debate. But none of them had been allowed to attend the meeting. They were our books, and we were their explicators. I took the picture home with me. It grew in my mind to an argument. I wanted a faculty meeting to be attended by as many black students as would be willing to come. I wanted them to talk to us. I wanted us to listen. How else could we understand what the hell was going on at the college?

Whatever else it was, my intention was also selfish. I wanted to be off my own hook. I needed to be relieved of those pictures I'd been creating in my mind, even if it had been deliberately and theatrically arranged for me to make them.

I proposed such a meeting to the dean of undergraduate studies, and he trotted over to the administration offices on its behalf. He was turned down. Those he'd spoken to feared for the safety of the faculty in such a gathering. The response astonished me. I was apppalled at this academic, clerkly ignorance of the circumstances under which physical violence could take place. But the absurdity of the institutional response relieved me of the more absurd parts of what had been my own imaginings. I was beginning to be open to other reactions. I was out of the jungle images.

A few days later I went to a meeting of the Academic Senate to which some representatives from the BSU had been invited—a compensation for the refusal to have black students at a faculty meeting. James Garrett spoke for them; the other four or five black students sat together at the side of the large room. Garrett was not much over twenty, slender, articulate, self-assured, and primed for the occasion. He addressed the senate for an uninterrupted half-hour. The suspensions had to be lifted—he emphasized that. The incident in the *Gater* offices he brushed over quickly. We didn't know the facts; he wasn't going to hint at them—and that was that. The rest of his talk was directed against the college's conditioned racism—the bureaucratic delays and bullshit when it came to doing something about Black Studies and the increased enrollment of black students. Garrett talked historically, he talked politically, he drawled, and he spoke rapidly. He jived too. He reminded us that the BSU had already told the academic vice-president that it would kick the man's ass if he didn't act for black students' needs. Garrett would tell the vice-president again, if he were here, that they'd kick his ass in.

I listened intently at first, but then I stopped hearing. I simply stared at him. Sometimes I turned away to stare at the other members of the BSU, whose silent presence reached me more than Garrett's talk. They were obviously aloof and sullen, and just a little tense—like reluctant witnesses at a hearing they scorned. Only when Garrett jived did they change their expressions. Then they threw their heads back, raised their arms, shook their palms, and laughed.

When Garrett finished, he remained at the front of the room fielding questions. I listened to about fifteen minutes of it. A professor of physical education, a former star basketball player with years of West Coast athletics behind him, and now a gray-haired, portly representative of his department in the Academic Senate, registered a sincere and baffled plaint. He didn't understand these accusations of racism. All athletes, regardless of color, had been just athletes to him. I winced. I didn't risk a glance toward Garrett's colleagues, but I heard the snickering. I raised my hand. Two minutes before that, I had no idea that I was going to speak.

I began by admitting that a month earlier I had refused to sign the petition for lifting the suspensions. I tried to explain why. I spoke about myself. I was looking at Garrett. Sometimes I looked at the other Blacks. They were all fixing their eyes on me. I said I didn't grow up a professor, I didn't read books in my boyhood. I had lived in ghettos, and when I lived in one with my own kind, I roamed streets, belonged to a gang. The incident in the *Gater* office, to me, was a gang thing. When I heard of it, my reaction was instinctive: get a bigger gang to go after the enemy. In the context of my present life, it simply and immediately meant suspensions. Now, having heard Garrett, I changed my mind. I would sign the petition. In itself, that wasn't an important thing. I was only one faculty member who'd changed his mind. The whole faculty needed to hear from Blacks, as the few of us had just heard. I asked them not to give up on faculty support. I asked the senate to call for a faculty meeting at which the black students could speak to us.

I must have puzzled colleagues who knew how adamant I'd been about not signing the petition. At home that evening I got calls from some of them who had attended the meeting and wanted to know what precisely impelled me to make the statement. Precisely, I could tell them nothing. It was how I felt, I said. They half expected I had some inside information I could share with them, or some concrete plan that would help resolve the conflicts. I had nothing. I enjoyed no great release that evening for what I had said, and I suffered no embarrassment. A few weeks later, at a faculty Christmas party, a member of the Academic Senate, referring to Garrett familiarly, said to me,. "I thought you had a clear head. Boy, did you get taken. I've heard Jimmy do that so many times now, I can go to sleep on it." And I couldn't answer, precisely, except to say—and mean it emphatically—"I didn't get taken."

I knew this. For years I'd been dead wrong to believe that any black student who happened into my classroom or office was an opportunity for me to demonstrate he was only a student, the same as any other. I had no such conviction. I always showed the lack of it with a slight excess of concern for him, with my unwillingness to be severe with him if his work was bad, and with my inability to let the word "Negro" ever drop between us unless he put it there. I was willing to admit all that now. He was not just a student whose skin happened to be black. He was a black man who happened to be a student. This trivial change required a major adjustment on my part. It took me out of a comfortable room into a place where I knew nothing. My words at the meeting had not been spoken out of guilt or fear, but out of my need for the help black students could give us. I wanted us to stop talking about them without them, and for this I needed, we needed, that they set aside that part of their militancy that was programmed for excluding me, us. And I imagined that our particular faculty, hearing the black students, seeing them, would want to move toward something that would help.

The faculty didn't meet with the black students. Christmas recess came, and in January, quietly, with a letter to the registrar, Summerskill lifted the suspensions. In January, too, Dr. Nathan Hare was hired to be the chairman of a Black Studies Program, or department, that didn't yet exist, but that he would, with encouraging promises from the administration, help to build. He was a black man in his early thirties, with a Ph.D. in sociology from the University of Chicago. He had also been a professional middleweight prize fighter. Some of us also knew that he had taught at Howard University, but had left, or been asked to. He was too militant for them; they were too Uncle Tom for him.

These two actions by Summerskill and the administration in January put an end to the black students' protests for that year. They were not prominently involved in the demonstrations during the spring semester of 1968. We heard that their leaders and Hare were busy planning for a Black Studies curriculum and for the increased enrollment of black students through the Equal Opportunities Program. White students who had supported the causes of the Blacks now turned to other causes: Vietnam; the Air Force R.O.T.C. on our campus; military-industrial recruiting; a Mexican-American professor "fired" from the History Department; and a clamor from a new student organization, calling itself the Third World Liberation Front, which wanted what the Blacks were apparently on their way to gaining. This organization with the grandiose title was composed mainly of students of Latin-American descent. Later, radical Oriental students came into it.

Whereas the Blacks arrived at open rebellion with one quick clout, the SDS-led spring operations pecked away most of the semester with jabs and bites: rallies, speeches, demonstrations, sit-ins and mill-ins. The police came from time to time. There were isolated instances of bloodletting. There were endless meetings, and a genuine effort by many members of the faculty, especially from the School of Humanities, to talk with dissenting students. The college was constantly in the headlines, and the messages from the governor, the chancellor, and the trustees were clear: Put your house in order, or we'll do it for you.

There were differences about "order." Pesident Summerskill resigned early in the spring. Liberal, eager to move with the college toward experimental possibilities, he was totally unprepared—as we all were—for what hit us as an unaccountable year. His resignation was to be effective as of September 1, but the trustees, near the close of the spring semester, at the height of a student demonstration, made the resignation effective immediately.

I learned through the spring that I had my own double standards. I was much more vulnerable to the anger and demands of black students than to those of radical whites who, more often than not, were engaged in symbolic, remote actions. The symbols didn't always correspond to my own, and what these students were willing to advocate often undermined what they were compelled to protest. Going after the military on campus by way of its pip-squeak R.O.T.C. was like denting fenders on the nearest Chevy because the board of General Motors was inaccessible. Also, those who cried loudest against R.O.T.C. and against Dow Chemical recruiting on campus would support courses in guerrilla warfare and the campus recruitment of sugar-cane cutters for Cuba. They could seize administration offices for one afternoon and make long-distance calls to Paris, London, Havana, New York— tilting back in swivel chairs and savoring cigars—and claim they were blowing my mind. But it required something else to move my mind to where it hadn't been before. In short, the black students had the advantage of being concrete. They wanted something better for themselves on the campus. White radicals wanted something better on campus and everywhere else.

In one intense academic year, the college's livable variety was suddenly intolerent and intolerable. The ingredients of the campus melting pot hardened. The students I had called hippies were, in my classes, turning into malcontents, the

activists into absentees, and the straights into puzzled ob-
servers of both. Most strongly I felt this erosion in a class on
Keats. The difficulties were never in the form of obvious
arguments about "relevance." Students could identify with
Keats' hurt life, and even with the set of abstractions to
which he had devoted his life—truth, beauty, imagination.
Their particular embodiments in the poetry, however, were
metaphors made difficult at times by campus action immediately preceding the class. Difficult for me, too. It called for a
fabulous purity of intention and an acrobatic turn of mind to
switch from the vocabulary of demonstrations and emergency faculty meetings to the vocabulary of bowers, nooks,
foxgloves, and nightingales.

Inevitably, the classroom itself became a theater for symbolic actions. One student wanted to know why I always
wore a tie to class. Another thought we'd gain community if
I stopped standing behind the table in front of the room and
sat with them in a circle of chairs. Term papers ought to be
abolished. Grades should be done away with. At times I
thought it was heartening that they could take the lid off and
speak so openly for what they wanted. At times I thought
they had gone mad to want it so much, for in itself it was
nothing.

By the end of that spring semester I was exhausted and
confused. Most of us were. None of us could any longer
clearly recall what had once been the spirit of the place. If
anything, the campus at S. F. State, in so short a time, had
become an emblem of the country itself. We fled toward our
summers seeking respite, but at the beginning of the summer, in California, Robert Kennedy was assassinated. At the
end of the summer, there was the Democratic Convention
in Chicago. The country had become a catastrophically en-
larged emblem of our campus, to which I limped back again

in the fall, unrecovered and still, for the even wilder year that lay ahead, unprepared.

During that summer Robert Smith, from the college's School of Education, an old hand at the politics of the campus, had been named president. As though he were to be baseball manager of a team whose success was uncertain, the appointment was limited to three years. And during that summer, George Murray, of the *Gater* incident, traveled around the state making Black Panther speeches. He was again scheduled by the English Department to teach in the fall, and he played his hand with that complication in mind. The chancellor of the state colleges, Glenn S. Dumke, was quick to call the hand. He had nothing to say to Murray, but plenty to Smith. At an English Department party that always opens the fall semester, and which Smith attended, Dumke phoned twice. The gist of it was: "Fire Murray." In essence, Smith replied that it was a matter of personnel, therefore an affair of the college only. Investigations were being made. Due process was to be assured. And to many of us at the party, Smith asserted that on this issue he would hold the line.

A Midwesterner with a phlegmatic manner, committee-room skills, and no gifts at all as a public speaker, Smith was headed for public spotlights. A resurgent BSU, claiming that college racism again thwarted their programs, would fire off the semester with speeches by Murray, Eldridge Cleaver, and Stokely Carmichael. Ronald Reagan, who had spent part of the summer as a serious Presidential possibility, responded immediately to the resumed campus noise. Chancellor Dumke, former President of S.F. State, former historian, former author of a potboiler novel entitled *The Tyrant of Baghdad*, would be the field marshall. Not in the field, of course, but at general headquarters in Los Angeles. From there he could talk confidently, just before it all began, of maintaining campus stability and peace through the use of force.

From *U. S. News & World Report*
September 23, 1968

Q. Dr. Dumke, will there be more riots on college campuses in the year ahead?

A. I believe this coming school year is going to be a year of even more widespread attempts at turbulence. But colleges and universities throughout the nation are much better able to cope with it.

In our California state college system, we're expecting all kinds of pressures for turbulence. But we now know better how to deal with these pressures.

Q. What gives you confidence that you will be able to cope with unrest any better than in the past?

A. We've had experience—we're "combat-ready." And we have made it absolutely clear that we are going to maintain the academic operation and integrity of our institutions with whatever force we have to apply to achieve it.

Our trustees have stated this policy with very clear-cut resolutions. Although we cannot guarantee calm, we can guarantee that, as far as our State Colleges are concerned, we will confront the serious issues facing us in an academic atmosphere of stability and peace.

5 · cowboys & indians

LEO LITWAK

I spoke to a colleague who was close to some of the BSU leaders. The students believed negotiations for a Black Studies Department had been deliberately prolonged. They felt there was a plot to sabotage the program by emasculating it. Could the black students have mistaken ordinary administrative red tape for sabotage? My friend thought the question irrelevant. They had waited too long. Unless the bureaucracy managed to come up with guaranteed assurances, the Blacks would assume that once again they had been tricked by negotiations that weren't meant to have any fruitful outcome.

My colleague told me that Dr. Nathan Hare, chairman of the proposed Black Studies Department, may have stumbled over bureaucratic details. But this, he felt, was only a convenient dodge by administrators who were extremely uncomfortable with the proposed department. They feared that they might be entering dangerous ground with a vague curriculum supervised by men who had expressed revolutionary sentiments. The bureaucrats—and my friend included a considerable number of the faculty in that designation—offered Dr. Hare almost no help in the confusing morass of paper work that even the most trivial curriculum matters entailed. Many of those responsible for authorizing the Black Studies Department were committed to an outmoded educational establishment, and this was the real basis for the black grievance. There was little sense of urgency among faculty and administration. They were busy with procedural problems when the times called for imaginative response. My friend said that the merits of the specific black complaints were irrelevant. It would be disastrous if the administration defended itself on the record and ignored the need for radical action. He believed every effort should have been made to spare the Black Studies Department from the bureaucratic quagmire ordinary programs had to traverse.

I made half-hearted attempts to find out about the proposed Black Studies curriculum. I learned some of the course designations—black psychology, black history—but I didn't pursue the matter. I had never been much involved in campus politics, and after a two-year absence from S.F. State, I was even less inclined to take them seriously. I felt that students exaggerated their power and their grievances. I regarded faculty politicians as operating in a provincial arena, distant from the real sources of power, their strategies petty, their impotence demonstrable and, therefore, embarrassing. I evaded extracurricular obligations. I remained detached from colleagues and students. I considered my real commitments to be elsewhere. This was a prejudice that became increasingly difficult to maintain as the crisis developed.

The center of campus—a green quadrangle—belonged to the students. A spine of giant evergreens ran part way down the center of the quad, aimed due west toward the commons, where the dining halls were located. Prefab huts, housing the BSU and the Associated Students, were at one side of the dining halls, the speaker's platform on the other side. The speaker's platform was the focal point of campus action. Here festivities and riots originated. I often stopped at the speaker's platform on my way to lunch. Standing on the periphery of the crowd, I listened a moment, then moved on, wishing I could be amused by a rhetoric that often made me uneasy.

One of the memorable events of early fall 1968 was the

appearance of Eldridge Cleaver, under the auspices of the Poetry Center. Six thousand students, assembled before the speaker's platform, filled the quad. Though introduced as a poet, Cleaver didn't intend anyone to define the conditions under which he would appear. He was not only the author of *Soul on Ice*—the basis for his poet's credentials—he was Minister of Infomation of the Black Panther Party, an editor of the radical *Ramparts* magazine, a paroled convict, and the Peace and Freedom Party's candidate for the United States Presidency. Presidential Candidate Cleaver was due to return to prison in early December as a parole violator. Eight years remained of a sentence for armed robbery. Cleaver had publicly announced that he would shoot it out with any officer who attempted to return him to prison. He told a friend of mine that since the night he watched Oakland police shoot down his fellow Panther, seventeen-year-old Bobby Hutton, he had himself felt half dead. Cornered with Bobby Hutton in a building, police had fired with gas grenades; he was injured when a grenade struck his leg. He stumbled naked into the open and surrendered. He watched police shoot down his young friend. According to Cleaver, they drove him through Oakland streets debating whether or not to kill him. The argument was resolved when the dispatcher informed the officers that the arrest was known and ordered Cleaver brought to the station for booking.

That fall day we heard more than poetry from the speaker's platform. The language Cleaver used was in itself a revolutionary act. He called San Francisco Police Chief Thomas Cahill a pig. He called Mayor Alioto a pig. Ditto Superintendent of Public Instruction Max Rafferty. He examined the ghetto significance of the word, "motherfucker." With its precise meaning established, he named his rivals for the United States Presidency "motherfuckers." He led several thousand students in a chant: "Fuck Reagan!"

A Berkeley professor who had supported the Free Speech Movement but had subsequently denounced radical students told me that he considered obscenity on campus—especially public obscenity—to be the most serious of all attacks on the academic community. He argued that our language was our currency. Debase the language and academic value was fatally compromised. Our language guaranteed our relations with each other and with our students. Our rituals and our prestige were grounded in manners secured by academic language. It was no accident that a man sounded professorial. More was involved than simply a snobbish pretense. If academic formalities were disregarded, we might quickly discover that there was no other bond that could glue together our divisions. We were one community only because language had made it so.

Cleaver tried to unmake it. He chose Governor Reagan as his essential opposition. He declared that he had never liked Reagan.

"Even back in the days of his bad movies—bullshit flicks that never turned me on to any glow—I felt about him the way I felt about such nonviolent cowboys as Roy Rogers and Gene Autry; that they were never going to cause any action or allow anything to happen. They were just there, occupying space and wasting my time, my money, and my sanity . . . One knew that movies were into a make-believe bag, but the unreality espoused on the screen by the flat souls of such pablum-fed actors as Reagan reflected to me—black ghetto nigger me—a sickening mixed bag of humorless laughter and perfect Colgate teeth, with never a real hint of the funk of life. Insipid, promising nothing and delivering even less, a Reagan movie was nothing to get excited about."

Cleaver offered hints as to the real funk of life. He wanted all nightmares exposed and all fantasies uttered. That was the sort of election campaign he intended to run.

" . . . this is the nightmare election year of the American Dream. Everything is out in the open this year. Nobody is trying very hard to conceal anything. As usual, the key issue in this election is what to do about the niggers . . . ,"

Cleaver was willing to let rage confront rage in a comic but deadly shoot-out. Addressing Reagan from the speaker's platform, he said, "I don't know what the outcome will be, but I do know that I, for one, will never kiss your ass, will never submit to your demagogic machinations. I think you are a cowardly, craven-hearted wretch. You are not a man. You are a punk. Since you have insulted me by calling me a racist, I would like to have the opportunity of balancing the books. All I ask is a sporting chance. Therefore, Mickey Mouse, I challenge you to a duel, to the death, and you can choose the weapons. And if you can't relate to that, right on. Walk, chicken, with your ass picked clean."

The challenge was comic and was intended to outrage. Cleaver ridiculed the cowboy legend of America. And yet I felt he meant the challenge seriously. "I think you are a cowardly, craven-hearted wretch." The real anger, undisguised by mockery, was for a moment exposed. He meant the slap in the face to sting. Later I heard other Blacks use the cowboy language in a mockery of Wild West myths that reflect so much of the American character. At the same time, I felt they were themselves guided by these myths. The Black Panther Party called on Blacks to arm themselves. They published a code of gallantry meant to govern their relations with each other and with the enemy. They weren't being funny either.

Cleaver appeared on campus just as the national elections reached their most intense heat. Superintendent of Public

Instruction Rafferty lagged far behind Democrat Alan Cranston in the Senate race. Rafferty—the enemy of philosopher John Dewey and progressive education and Vietnam doves and namby-pamby professors—was Reagan's man all the way.

Governor Reagan had received political advantage from campus unrest. His large plurality in the 1966 gubernatorial election was generally attributed to his reaction to the Free Speech Movement at Berkeley, which initiated the pattern of university upheaval. Reagan had reflected the majority attitude when he assailed the students as irresponsible children in need of discipline. He said at the time of the first Berkeley demonstrations, "It is the penalty we pay for appeasement. When that police car was surrounded and the police were roughed up by students and nonstudents, university officials should have restored order, even to expelling students. At bottom was the fact that the administration abandoned all rules concerning student conduct. I don't subscribe to that." He attributed campus excesses to the vacillation of irresolute administrators and the encouragement of radical faculty. He had more than once criticized the political imbalance of university and college faculties, which privileged the left and deprived conservatives of any effective influence. He saw colleges and universities as hotbeds of liberalism. He said that radical students abused an education to which they had no inherent right. Higher education, he later said, was a privilege. At a time when state budgets were running out of hand and a significant part of the budget was used up by education, he demanded that students pay their way in what had hitherto been a tuition-free system. He largely based his successful campaign on hostility toward the intellectual community, which the public shared.

It's irrelevant to question Reagan's sincerity. His inclinations undoubtedly corresponded with what was politically expedient. A large part of the public was more than willing to find professor and student at the origin of the nation's failure. The peace movement, draft resistance, ghetto riots, crime on the streets—these were all considered preludes to the violation of that ultimate American sanctuary, the campus. The campus had special appeal to the public as a place where childhood could be prolonged, and our legendary life enshrined and celebrated. Even those who had never made it beyond high school regarded the sweetheart of Sigma Chi, Saturday afternoon football, Friday night warm-ups, beery high jinx at the fraternity house, and Mr. Chips as a part of their own history. They wanted this dreamy, golden way of life to remain inviolate. They needed assurance that there was some comparable payoff for their own lives. The cry for revolution was overheard as a threat to that golden moment everyone had vainly struggled for. Many citizens believed their lives would go down the drain if the prize were declared to be worthless and contemptible.

Reagan was the reflection of this public view. He articulated perhaps more effectively than any other politician the growing consensus that saw the radical-professor-student-Black as the beast in America's jungle.

Obscenity on campus raped an American fantasy enshrined by Hollywood movies.

I had the sense listening to Cleaver—having read his book and some of his articles—that there was nothing simple or innocent in his intelligence. Reagan may be no more than he manifests himself to be. He may have paid the price of his years in Hollywood and television and become no more than his roles—really a conservative, really a rancher, really a gubernatorial candidate, and now, really a governor. He may indeed have become superficial, lucid, honest, sincere, glued together by a simple conservative dogma. Cleaver, however, impressed me as the master of a mode of dialectical confrontation that had gained currency among the California avantgarde. There was a growing movement that regarded education and therapy as linked processes, transcending language, aiming at heightened awareness. Many of the students listening to Cleaver had attended the Experimental College, where the Reichian-oriented encounter techniques developed by Esalen Institute had great influence. Cleaver, emphasizing the need for a new integration of mind and body, imagined that a confrontation of white and black would bring it about.

His dialectical temper was in tune with radical college youth. There was diminishing respect for the therapeutic and educational function of precise language. There was growing irritation with the professor committed to an academic language. There was a movement toward a more Reichian objective, language being used as one of various means for discovering contradictions and impasses in order to remove numbing inhibitions. So there was considerable support—not only among the radicals and the hippies, but among the advocates of the Experimental College—for using language provocatively, even dangerously. That was Cleaver's style. Reagan represented the other extreme. His public manner was utterly safe and devoid of risk. He operated from the security of indubitable premises with which he was thoroughly familiar. His most common tone toward anyone who challenged his variety of conservatism was a grimacing forbearance. Reagan allowed no room for surprises. He also offered none. This undoubtedly charmed a public seeking just such an air of conviction in times that permitted little clarity and no safety. Reagan was perfectly oriented in every debate. He never ventured far from home. He had decisive attitudes toward the ghetto because he had never visited the ghetto. He had firm prescriptions for Vietnam precisely because he had never seen a battlefield off a movie set. He knew exactly how to deal with higher education even though his own education had not moved beyond four years at Eureka College in the early thirties. And he knew how campus turmoil should be managed because he never ventured on to a campus except under the careful guard of his security forces during board meetings. Reagan was so clear because he was out of touch.

The duel Cleaver demanded will never come to pass. The ex-con from the ghetto doesn't operate in the same arena with the man who writes nostalgically of his childhood as having been a Mark Twain existence. They live in separate enclaves. They use language differently and are prepared for different sorts of risks. Reagan would never care to venture into Cleaver terrain, nor Cleaver into his. The Black Panther argument, in fact, is that the melting pot has never worked, that ethnic groups continue to occupy separate strata in the social hierarchy: white Protestant Anglo-Saxon on top, the Irish, Italians, Jews, etc., somewhere in between, the black man on the bottom. The Panthers argue that since no one vacates his power willingly, the black man must demand—violently, if necessary—his rightful place.

Cleaver climaxed his brilliant and obscene speech at S.F. State by chanting, "Power to the people. Black power to black people, red power to red people, yellow power to yellow people, student power to students, faculty power to faculty. Yes. Even to faculty—if they want it."

If Reagan wanted to exploit incidents to benefit conservative candidates in the coming elections, Cleaver and fellow Panther George Murray were more than willing to oblige.

Cleaver was Black Panther Minister of Information; Murray, Minister of Education. Whatever the difference in function, there was a difference in tone. Cleaver was subtle, complicated, ironic. Threat was mixed with comedy. He entertained you as he assaulted you. George Murray wasn't devious. The education he offered was made brutally plain, unmixed by entertainment.

From the moment officials of the state became aware that George Murray had been rehired by the English Department of San Francisco State College, there were outraged protests, orchestrated by Max Rafferty, who had made it clear that he would himself use tough, old-fashioned methods in controlling campus disorders.

In his office as Black Panther Minister of Education, George Murray traveled to various state campuses and spoke bloody revolution to the multitudes. In a speech delivered at Fresno State College, he called Reagan, Nixon, and George Wallace "insane buffoons." The speech was entitled "The Necessity for Black Revolution." Murray made it clear that the revolution he had in mind was to be armed and violent. "We maintain," said Murray, as if quoting from Mao's *Little Red Book*, "that political power comes through the barrel of a gun." He went on to say, "And if you want campus autonomy, if the students want to run the college, if the cracker administration don't go for it, then you control it with the gun." There was little subtlety in his style, only plain speech. "We are slaves and the only way to become free is to kill the slave masters."

For Max Rafferty, Murray was a tailor-made villain. The polls indicated that Rafferty wasn't closing the gap in his Senate race with Cranston. With the pot boiling at S.F. State, a little more heat might have caused it to spill over before election time. President Smith resisted Rafferty's demand that Murray be suspended. He said that charges brought against Murray on the basis of his incendiary campus speeches were under investigation and the college intended to follow its established grievance procedures.

The week preceding the elections, Murray—obviously disdaining the complaints of Rafferty and Reagan—climbed on a table in the commons dining hall and summoned all Blacks to listen to him. He announced a BSU strike for the following week. He urged the Blacks to carry guns. His precise advice has been disputed. He himself claims that he instructed Blacks to carry guns at all times—not merely on campus—in order to defend themselves from the murderous assault of "pigs."

According to a student of mine, George Murray, standing on a table, was an intimidating presence. He rallied the Blacks and ignored the Whites.

His style at the time seemed characteristic of other Black Panthers. Head tilted to the side, eyes squinting, face wrinkled in a grimace, he gave forth his virulent message with a singsong delivery.

When Chancellor Dumke, a Reagan supporter, ordered President Smith to suspend Murray immediately for the tabletop call to arms, Smith refused. He called Dumke's order unprecedented. It would interrupt the due process to which Murray had a right. Smith consulted with Mayor Alioto. It was widely suspected that the intrusion of Republican state officials in a campus grievance procedure was directly connected with the coming elections. Mayor Alioto urged that instead of suspending Murray, the city be allowed to discover some violation of law so that proceedings against Murray would not involve college officials, who were barely able to keep the lid on the campus. The chancellor remained adamant, and the mayor asked that the decision at least be delayed until after Halloween, an especially taxing night for the police.

Clearly, it was everyone's expectation that the suspension of George Murray would produce a violent reaction from the Black Students Union.

When, on November 2, President Smith suddenly acceded to the chancellor and suspended Murray, the San Francisco State faculty was caught by surprise. Why hadn't he taken his stand against the intrusion of state politics? If any issue could have united the faculty, it was resentment of Chancellor Dumke's awkward bureaucratic manner which had so often failed to consider what the faculty regarded as its rights.

Few of us had anticipated Smith's sudden yielding to the chancellor. It was an act that divided the faculty and signaled the various factions on campus to begin their confrontation. The confrontation was quick in coming—but not until after Rafferty's defeat by Cranston on election day.

Black Student Union
DEMANDS AND EXPLANATIONS

1.–That all Black Studies courses being taught through various other departments be immediately part of the Black Studies Department and that all the instructors in this department receive full-time pay.

Explanation: At the present time the so-called Black Studies courses are being taught from the established departments which also control the function of courses. In order for a brother or sister to teach a Black Studies course he or she has to go before the assigned department head to receive permission to teach, which clearly shows that the power lies with the departments and the racist administrators, not with the Black Studies Department chairman, faculty and staff.

At the end of the summer before the fall of '68, the racist administration announced that 47 full-time teaching positions were unfilled. The Black Studies Department only receives 1.2 teaching positions out of the total number of 47. The Black Studies Department instructors should receive full-time pay like the various other departments on the San Francisco State College campus.

2.–That Dr. Hare, chairman of the Black Studies Department, receive a full professorship and a comparable salary according to his qualifications.

Explanation: Dr. Hare is one of the best sociologists in the country and one of the most sought-after, yet he makes less money than any department chairman and all newly appointed deans and administrators.

3.–That there be a Department of Black Studies which will grant a Bachelor's degree in Black Studies; that the Black Studies Department chairman, faculty and staff have the sole power to hire and fire without the interference of the racist administration and the chancellor.

4.–That all unused slots for Black students from fall 1968 under the Special Admissions Program be filled in spring 1969.

Explanation: The 128 slots that were not filled by so-called "special admittees" should be filled by any Third World students who wish to attend San Francisco State College in spring 1969.

5.–That all Black students who wish to, be admitted in fall 1969.

Explanation: In San Francisco 70 percent of all primary, junior-high and high-school students are Third World, but at S.F.S.C. only 4 percent of the entire student body are Third World students. In other words the racist pig power structure does not want an abundance of "niggers" in their so-called "institutions of higher learning."

6.–That twenty (20) full-time teaching positions be allocated to the Department of Black Studies.

Explanation: At the beginning of the fall semester, 1.2 percent teaching positions were allocated to the so-called Black Studies Department. How in hell can a department function with such a small number of teaching positions?

7.–That Dr. Helen Bedesem be replaced in the position of Financial Aid Officer and that a Black person be hired to direct it and that Third World people have the power to determine how it will be administered.

Explanation: Helen Bedesem represents the old ante-bellum plantation mistress, the showpiece of the slavemaster who decides what the field niggers need and don't need. We want her replaced with a Third World person who is absolutely responsible to Third World and poor students, not a house nigger, Uncle Tom, Tio Taco or a Charlie Chan.

8.–That no disciplinary action will be administered in any way to any students, workers, teachers or administrators during and after the strike as a consequence of their participation in the strike.

Explanation: the racist administration should not threaten the security and well-being of people who support and participate in the strike.

9.–That the California State College trustees not be allowed to dissolve any Black programs on or off the San Francisco State College campus.

Explanation: On November 22-24, the California State College trustees will meet at the request of Pig Dumke to dissolve the

Associated Students on all state college campuses throughout the state. This means that we cannot create and maintain programs on and off campus. Everything we do will be controlled by the Pig Dumke. All programs such as the Associated Students, CSI, EC, etc., will have to have Pig Dumke's O.K. If the trustees destroy our creativity on campus and off campus, we will use our creativity in a prolonged and protracted war against them.

10.–That George Murray maintain his teaching position on this campus for the 1968-1969 academic year.

Explanation: George Murray is one of the best English instructors on the campus. He was fired not because of his teaching activity but because of his political philosophy. This is insane and absurd and he must be reinstated to continue to educate and enlighten the Third World students in his class.

6 · the hunger for clarity

LEO LITWAK

I wasn't on campus the day the BSU strike began. The event had been long advertised. It promised, at the very least, to be an exciting show. It was perhaps a measure of my alienation that I didn't as yet see it as my show. I didn't consider the possibility that I might myself be on stage. Instead, I prepared to muffle all shocks with a distancing irony.

I went that day to a different spectacle, the funeral of a man who had been a casual acquaintance. The setting was a hillside above the ocean. The burial ground was ringed with eucalyptus and redwood. The burial party was composed of that heterogeneous assembly of occupations, religions, dress styles, hair styles, life styles which had come to characterize Bay Area sacraments.

Why do I insist on this tone of irony? The young man who had died had seemed unusually graced. He mastered whatever he tried. He had been a ski instructor, he was an expert sailor, a first-rate carpenter. He founded a chain of restaurants, and before he was thirty, had become financially independent. He was part of the mainstream. His family was rooted in middle-class America and perhaps this troubled him. They were at the center of myths a new generation regarded as its nightmares. This young man was weary of his achievements. He no longer received a charge from his business success. His marriage had failed. He began a desperate hunt for a new revelation. He tried encounters at Esalen Institute. He attended Sexual Freedom League parties. He dropped acid. His fervent desire for self-transcendence ended in an overdose of sleeping pills.

I summarized his life and death too neatly, no doubt to remain untouched by his dying. I came to his funeral as to a spectacle.

The middle-aged, craggy-featured minister who presided seemed out of place in such exotic company. He stood by the grave side in his blue serge suit, and then surprised me by slighting scripture for the writings of Plato and Kahlil Gibran, favorites, he explained, of the dead man. The family, too, seemed old-fashioned and out of place. The father was himself a minister. He and his wife might have stood for a Norman Rockwell portrait. Yet when they greeted me as if they assumed I loved their son and shared their grief, I couldn't maintain my distant focus or hold to the caricature I tried to impose on them. As the casket lowered, they collapsed into the arms of their other son, a burly giant who might have stepped from the ranks of the Tac Squad. He had the awkward, powerful figure of a cop. He was dressed square. It was no use seeing him as a cop, however. He hugged his shattered parents, and I couldn't stay out of his shoes or deny my own impulse to weep.

So, the sacrament of burial worked as it usually does, despite all innovations, joining the congregation—however heterogeneous—in a vision of a common destiny. All our differences seemed irrelevant.

Later that day I heard that the BSU had "run amuck" and forced the campus to shut down, and I felt they were attacking the people to whom I had become reconciled at the funeral. I saw the possibility of a grieving son in every cop and a suffering father in every thin-lipped, plain-spectacled administrator. Television gave me a sensational report of events at San Francisco State College. Headlines confirmed my sudden antipathies. I damned the cruel students for denying the humanity of the Establishment. Hearing the reports of that day, I welcomed the cops. But within a few days my feelings were reversed. I no longer saw sons and fathers among the helmeted, visored blue-coats with their yard-long clubs. It was the cops I wanted off campus.

These emotional flip-flops continued throughout the strike, destroying my efforts to find unshakable ground.

There was nothing secret about the BSU strategy. For weeks they had broadcast their intentions from the speaker's platform and throughout the commons. They declared against the strategy which, until that point, had characterized campus demonstrations. They didn't intend to invade buildings and pen themselves up until police arrested them. They quoted Mao's *Little Red Book* and threatened guerrilla warfare. They warned that they wouldn't march docilely into concentration camps like "good Jews." They would maneuver outside buildings, evading the strength of their enemies. They made vague but ominous threats of bombs and guns.

The day before the strike, November 5, Stokely Carmichael addressed the BSU in the Main Auditorium. No whites were allowed. The few who tried to enter were pummeled and cast out. Carmichael urged the students to stick to the general principle of the strike, which was to "gain control of one's own destiny." Their demands, he told them, were designed to free them from the power that enslaved them.

November 6 was the anniversary of the purported assault by George Murray and others on the office of the student newspaper. The choice of that day to begin the strike indicated that the BSU had decided to exploit the image of violent and dangerous intruders imposed on them by newspaper accounts. The bulk of the BSU rank and file—four hundred students enrolled under a special admissions program—had come directly from ghetto streets, suspicious of college customs and surely not yet seduced by blandishments of academic success. They didn't have middle-class reservations about violence.

After a pep talk in the auditorium, the black students broke up into small bands and scattered to all parts of the campus. They swept through corridors, howling, banging on doors, overturning trash cans, shattering glass.

An IBM typewriter was heaved through an office window.

A large bookcase was toppled in an office.

The equipment in a science lab was damaged.

A few days later, black students wearing stocking masks entered the Anthropology Department office and cut the cord of an electric typewriter.

They invaded classrooms, erased lessons from black-boards, writing instead: ON STRIKE. CLASS DISMISSED.

They commanded all classes to cease immediately.

For those who resisted their command, the experience could be humiliating. A professor of business told me, "They came into the room, interrupted my lecture, announced the strike, ordered us to leave the room. When no one moved, they grabbed some girls in the front row and pulled them toward the door. I could see that the male students were upset and that there might be a fight. So I told the Blacks they could have fifteen minutes to present their case. Instead, they warned us that another group was coming to enforce the strike order and they left. But there was no further disruption."

Another group entered a biology classroom. When the teacher refused to cooperate, they erased the lesson, surrounded him, and jabbed him with umbrellas. The teacher giggled. The classroom quickly emptied.

A photo was published in a student newspaper showing an English professor grimly seated in his classroom in the middle of a group of Blacks led by Dr. Nathan Hare, head of the Black Studies Program. Dr. Hare, a professional boxer, was an intimidating presence.

And so it went for an hour, until the Tac Squad arrived to clear the campus.

President Smith immediately issued a statement denying that the black students had legitimate grounds for a strike. "The record is clear that the college has moved more rapidly in support of Black Studies at San Francisco State than it has on any other program in recent years." He described the steps taken and then complained that the impressive record of achievement had been unfairly characterized as "foot-dragging and a racist effort to destroy the whole concept of Black Studies." He said that he had not seen the ten demands until the day before the strike. The BSU had presented them in a news conference to which the president was not invited. "Yesterday, on the eve of the strike, the demands were presented to me and to the deputy president at 4:00 P.M. by a committee of seven. I was asked to agree to them on the spot. I was told that the strike would proceed in any event." The BSU described their demands as "nonnegotiable." They didn't want to talk.

Smith was determined to keep the campus open for instruction. He said that he would employ whatever police force was necessary to do the job. So the confrontation became a familiar one. Police arrived on campus. Uniformed officers remained out of sight. Presumably inconspicuous plain-clothes men were posted at entrances to buildings and in corridors. Some wore hippy clothes and beards. There was little art to their disguise and students frequently discovered them. Even I could make them out when they resembled middle-aged jocks in pullover sweaters, text books pressed under their arms. They were stationed at building entrances and other strategic points and didn't budge.

On the second day of the strike, a bull horn summoned all those in the commons to assemble in front of the speaker's platform. Those who entered the cafeteria for lunch were scolded. "Food is not where it's at," the black speaker said. "We' re shutting this campus down. If this school don't function for us, then it's not going to operate."

A BSU speaker, using the amplifying system on the speaker's platform, urged the substantially white crowd to join the strike. "We have to keep this school shut down. We shall escalate our activities. This strike must move to a mass basis, not only black and Third World, but also white. Our actions are being followed by students all over the country and in Europe. We are part of a world-wide movement. Two hundred and sixty-six brothers died in Mexico." He had an audience of several thousand students. No police were in view. But they were around. A black student, carrying a walkie-talkie, rushed up and talked to the speaker, who then gave the message to the crowd: "I understand there are pigs on campus." He drew the word PIGS out to several syllables. The crowd included a core of some three or four hundred—mainly white—who responded enthusiastically, chanting slogans on cue.

"We are many and the pigs are few," the speaker said. "When we have them isolated, we will strike. When they assemble to attack, we shall disperse." The speaker told the crowd to remember the tactics of Mao and not be afraid. He told them not to be deceived by the liberal words of President Smith, who, after all, worked for the "corporate interests."

An excited young lady rushed toward the platform, shouting, "The pigs are in the Humanities Building!"

A group of students—both black and white—surrounded two men at the rear of the crowd. They didn't look like policemen to me. One was an Oriental. They were of medium height, indistinguishable from students. They were obviously frightened as the crowd pressed around them, oinking and jeering. They moved toward the end of the commons where the classroom buildings were located. At the end of the walk, an entire line of plain-clothes men materialized and absorbed the two.

Violence during the next few days was of a sophomoric nature. Fires were set in restroom trash cans. Toilets were plugged. Nonetheless, the striking students encouraged the feeling that we were on the edge of homicide.

I was informed that white allies of the BSU would come to our classrooms to explain the strike. Still outraged by the initial violence, I prepared for the intrusion by rehearsing an argument against the cowboy mentality that made its case by force of arms. I nervously considered what my response would be if I were treated with disrespect in front of my class. This triggered off cowboy fantasies of my own. The radical who arrived to "educate" my class turned out to be one of my students. The week before, he had solicited my opinion of his writing. Now he had arrived very respectfully to lecture me. He wore a red arm band. His long hair was knotted in back. His bandit mustache gave him the appearance of a villainous swashbuckler in an Errol Flynn period movie.

The class protested his justification of the ten demands. Some students argued that the demands had separatist implications, especially the demand for free and open admissions for all black students, regardless of qualifications. Others confessed that they were sympathetic to the black demands but they rejected the violent tactics of the strike.

The strike emissary admitted that he, too, had doubts concerning some of the specific demands, but the basic issue seemed clear to him and he didn't intend to quibble. We were, he said, a racist institution in a racist society, and only revolutionary change could correct that situation. As for the purported acts of violence committed by the Blacks, these were trivial compared with the injuries inflicted on black people for four hundred years. He accused white society of practicing genocide against the Blacks.

A girl student who had been involved in radical politics since the days of the Free Speech Movement at Berkeley complained she was tired. After the ideological fervor subsided, apathy had set in and now she was sick of revolutionary cant. She just wanted to do her work, get her degree, and get out.

The entire campus blossomed with groups debating the virtues of the strike. At noon, radical speakers—black and white—addressed the crowd from the speaker's platform. Placards appeared all over the commons, bearing the slogans which in the next months were to become the clichés of a national movement: ON STRIKE, SHUT IT DOWN. EITHER YOU'RE PART OF THE SOLUTION OR YOU'RE PART OF THE PROBLEM. Instead of correcting misspellings of "fascist" and "racist" the new spellings—as if they implied new meanings—became standard: "FACIST," "RASCIST." The demands were posted everywhere as though they were the Ten Commandments. A giant banner crossed the façade of the dining room, proclaiming the strike.

It became obvious in the first week of the strike that white radical students had been assigned proselytizing and educating duties by the BSU. Picket lines formed at entrances to classroom buildings in the late morning and early afternoon. They were led by SDS captains who tried, by bull horn incantation, to close the school.

Booths were set up around the commons and in the various courtyards in front of classroom buildings. Broadsides, strike newspapers, campus newspapers, position papers of various student organizations were distributed.

By the third day, several other ethnic minorities entered the strike under the banner of the Third World Liberation Front, an amalgam of Mexican-American, Oriental, Filipino, and American Indian organizations. Their five demands were tacked onto the original ten of the BSU. The strikers now demanded an autonomous School of Ethnic Studies which would incorporate separate ethnic departments.

BSU leader Jack Alexis, addressing a School of Humanities faculty meeting, proclaimed that the fifteen demands were only the beginning of the revolution, not its end. All students had grievances, he said, not merely the ethnic minorities. Once the current issues were settled, others would arise. The revolution would challenge every feature of the college in its pursuit of a "relevant education." "Don't think," Alexis warned us, "that you're going to solve this strike and then return to normal. This college may never again return to normal."

The administration responded to the wealth of strike literature with a single memorandum that attempted a point-by-point response to the demands. The rebuttal was stiff, impersonal, sluggish with bureaucratic jargon. The fifteen demands—according to the administration memorandum—had either never before been submitted for negotiation or were already in the process of being satisfied. Some of them, however, were simply beyond the power of the college to grant.

President Smith delayed in responding to a faculty petition calling for a general assembly. We were told—off the record—that there had been bomb threats and it would be hazardous to assemble the faculty in one place. The campus chapter of the American Federation of Teachers moved to overcome the faculty inertia. It represented a minority of the faculty, at most two or three hundred; although its leadership was militant, its rank and file was generally inactive.

The day before the strike, the executive council of the union issued a statement in support of the BSU:

> The executive council of the A.F.T. met yesterday, November 4, in an emergency session and unanimously passed the following resolution: "Recognizing the validity of many grievances of the Black Students Union, and recognizing the extreme violation of all due process and right governance of an academic community, as indicated by Chancellor Dumke's dictatorial action with regard to George Murray, we therefore support the strike presently called for, we urge individual union members to act in support of the proposed strike, and we call for the resignation of Chancellor Dumke, who has proven himself no longer a reputable member of the academic community."

I attended a union meeting at Ecumenical House across the street from the campus. The membership was so divided by this statement with its outright support of the BSU that the union played no effective part in the crisis for the next several weeks.

The Economics Department had meanwhile circulated an announcement that seemed a more promising ground for faculty initiative:

> The members of the Department of Economics unanimously recommend that the faculty at large go on strike (not meet classes) in protest against Chancellor Dumke's interference in the due process of S.F. State College in the Murray affair. Those departments thinking of taking a similar stand are invited to meet selected members of the Department of Economics at 10 A.M., Friday, November 8, in HLL 141, to discuss strategy and iron out differences in proposals.

Since no reference was made to the student strike, this proposal seemed to provide a basis for faculty consensus.

An ad hoc committee was formed and almost immediately raised a strike motion.

I argued against the motion, urging instead a general convocation to clarify the issues. My political education lagged far behind that of those who were present. They had tried convocations. The administration allowed talk to go on and on. When it was over, the machinery was turned on again and nothing was changed.

The mood of the ad hoc committee was summarized by a psychology professor who said, "Sooner or later we'll have to strike, and we'll never have a better occasion than now. Let's get our feet wet. If we don't move now, they'll justifiably dismiss us as ridiculous."

A statement was published on November 10. It contained, in part, the following:

> On Friday morning a number of faculty members met at the unanimous invitation of the Economics Department to discuss a strike "in protest against Chancellor Dumke's interference in the due processes of S.F. State College in the Murray affair." We oppose the suspension as symptomatic of long and continued interference with autonomy of the college. If the chancellor does not rescind his order to suspend Murray by Tuesday at 5 P.M., the ad hoc committee plans to strike Wednesday morning.

BSU leader Nesbitt Crutchfield appeared at the ad hoc committee meeting to urge us not to offer so narrow a basis for a strike. He said that George Murray was only marginal to the interests of the BSU. "What is basically involved is that we of the black community gain control of our own destiny. Our demand is for self-determination and that demand is nonnegotiable. If black students and faculty control the Black Studies Department, then the issue of George Murray is irrelevant, for we alone will decide who is to be hired and who fired."

I accompained a group from the ad hoc committee that delivered the strike resolution to President Smith.

I had never met Smith before. He impressed me as an honest man, squeezed by contradictions I couldn't myself have resolved if I were in his place. He appreciated our effort to support him. He felt we were misguided and were, in fact, increasing the pressure on his office. It was his intention to keep the campus going until passions were eased and workable alternatives to the present impasse emerged. We learned that he had acceded to Dumke's order suspending Murray because he was considering the same action himself. He assured us that Murray would receive full pay while under suspension. Smith was opposed to any strike action and warned us of the consequences, especially in the light of a state law requiring the "resignation" of any state employee who was absent without leave for five successive days.

The students, meanwhile, flooded the campus with strike literature. They provided a history of the Experimental College and its relation to the Black Studies Program. They described a proposal before the state legislature that would modify the State Code in order to suppress the Experimental College. They published monographs on the question of violence. They simply outmatched the commonplace talents of the administration press resources. The students offered a history of the college and the changes wrought by the Master Plan adopted in 1960. They analyzed the board of trustees, providing biographies and political connections of all board members. Chinese students issued a monograph on the Chinese ghetto, which detailed the failure of the city and the college to meet the needs of their community.

The students continued discussing the strike everywhere. Much of the discussion was remarkably accomplished. A little of it was incendiary and idiotic. For instance, I heard a white student express his desire to blow up the Humanities Building. He was cautioned against the act by another white student who argued that the bombs might kill a black man. "If there's one black man in that building we have no right to blow it up."

The other answered—assuming a black voice for the purpose—"If he's in there, then he's an ass kisser. Let him burn."

"Maybe he's in there because he's reading about John Brown," the other responded.

The white students held open strategy meetings in the Gallery Lounge. Everyone was welcome. These meetings were usually conducted at an impressive level but there was occasional foolishness. I observed a young white man of bookish appearance in proletarian costume address the crowd in a black man's voice. "I know there are some motherfuckin' finks in this crowd. I don't care if the pigs listen to what I got to say. I say, enough of talk. You can make your plans about picketing but I'll do my own thing. There are a lot of buildings on this campus. And some of us cats want to see them go down." The students ignored him as if he were an embarrassment.

The black students remained aloof, except for their leaders, who addressed large meetings of faculty and students. The issue of violence was intensely discussed by their white supporters. In accepting the BSU policies, the students developed a rationale for violence more or less summarized in a broadside worth quoting at length.

WHO'S BEING VIOLENT . . . Everybody's against violence, but damn few people know what it is or what it means or why it happens.

The fact is, there are certain kinds of violence we live with every day. We're so accustomed to them that we think of them as normal, inevitable. That's the subtle violence of manipulation and exploitation, of isolation, of indifference to human suffering, our own included. It's the violence that channels us through school, makes us grub for grades, write theses, get our B.A. and our job with IBM and our two-car garage, that makes us lead a boring, useless, meaningless life and keeps us from realizing that there could be any alternatives, that any other kind of world could possibly exist. The only reason all this isn't imposed through physical force is because it isn't necessary. They don't need to butcher us; we're so full of self-hate that we'll do the job ourselves.

Black people have reached the point where they've abandoned that self-hate. It's partly because they aren't shielded from reality the way we are; they feel violence and coercion that is overt, vicious, openly brutal. They see an educational system bent on destroying their own culture, denying their identity, keeping them in their place, depriving them of a REAL education, relevant to their needs. They grow up in abominable ghetto schools where the only things taught are hate and fear and subservience; they come to college—those that are permitted—and are lectured on the importance of becoming white. Black Studies? There "isn't enough money." (Dick Gregory used to say, "When the economy's going to tighten its belt, who do you think gets the first notch?") George Murray? He said a four-letter word, "guns." Do you have a grievance? Don't make waves; the college structure is very delicate and mustn't be upset.

So black students realized that their survival was at stake. They realized that this college had to come to a grinding halt if they weren't to be slowly destroyed. And they couldn't count on white students who weren't as hip to the situation as they were to close it down for them. They are only a minority. And yet they had to protect themselves from extinction. So they engaged in a little disruption. Not much, mind you—the kind of "disruption" that took place yesterday looks pretty innocuous in the face of the advent of the Tactical Squad, fondling their tear gas canisters and night sticks. The real disruption of the education process (what little there is) came from Chancellor Dumke and the trustees, bent on crushing the black and white student programs like Tutorial . . . Experimental College . . . Special Admissions . . . the student anti-war movement, that have tried to show that alternatives to the trustees' world of racism, fear, and repression do exist. They engaged in a little disruption, and with a minimum of violence, without serious confrontation with police, without a lot of people getting arrested or hurt, they succeeded in shutting the place down. They put the heat back on the people who are responsible for all this, the people on the top.

The analysis of violence was further evidence of the encounter orientation that the Experimental College had promoted. It was an analysis concerned as much with the fear of violence as with the act of violence. The fear, often disproportionate to the threat, suggested a pathological condition. People, armored in preparation for any assailant, were made invulnerable to deep feeling. In such cases, it might be therapeutic to prescribe violent confrontation. Guerrilla theater and street psychodrama become means of therapy as well as revolution. Many of the radical students saw revolution as therapy. They considered effective education as also therapeutic and therefore revolutionary. One achieved guarantee against violence only at the sacrifice of his education and his capacity for joy.

The black man was viewed as still having heroic possibilities, because he couldn't escape violence or deep feeling. Street education had its advocates on campus. The black man appeared to the white radical student in the guise of revolutionary instructor and therapist. His acts of violence were viewed as rational. Black violence which educated and liberated was contrasted to police violence whose intention was to inhibit.

The students—black and white—almost immediately deepened the issues of the confrontation so that the demands became the symbolic representation of a larger cause. Higher education was to be entirely transformed. Everything. The relationship of instructor to student, the determination of curriculum, the relationship of campus to community. The revolutionary argument denied that an educational establishment could remain uncommitted to vital issues.

A young man, sitting in front of the commons, was introduced to me as a leader of the Young Socialist Alliance. I questioned him about the radical strategy of using the campus as a staging ground for revolution. At that time Herbert Marcuse articulated the ideology which radical students generally accepted. He had spoken in opposition to campus revolution. He said that the campus was in need of reform but that he had little confidence in the improvisations that would replace the university. In fact, he valued the American university above the European. It was his position that the campus was still a place where intellectuals could remain alienated from the technological society. The young man shrugged off these ideological considerations.

"I don't agree with Marcuse on that. If there can be no adequate education for Blacks, then there must be no education for anyone."

This was the most strongly held conviction among the students, moderate and radical. They refused to thrive in a system which inhibited black culture and black power. To participate in the fruits of a racist system was to be a racist, whatever good intentions one declared.

White students readied themselves to undergo what black men had suffered, anticipating their own revolutionary transformation.

I didn't want the violence of the street to penetrate the campus. Perhaps it was true that so long as we were ignorant of street life there would inevitably be something hypocritical in our academic experience. Violence was as American as apple pie, as German as strudel, as Polish as kubase, as Italian as spaghetti, as English as Yorkshire pudding, as Russian as borscht, as Nigerian as yams. It was the ordinary condition of the world's peasantry and proletariat. Even we professors knew that. Many of us had come to the campus to escape that condition.

The English professor surrounded by Blacks who interrupted his class to announce the strike was a refugee from the Nazis. Until the strike, he was safe on campus. And I was safe. Why didn't the Blacks jump on board alongside us instead of rocking the boat? They wanted full autonomy for a Black Studies Department, including "the sole power to hire faculty and determine the destiny of its department." They were, in fact, demanding power that no other department on campus possessed. I sympathized with their indictment of the curriculum, which I, too, believed had no inherent logic but merely reflected the aggrandizement over decades of established academic empires. Great efforts had been made to accommodate student needs without sacrificing established power. And these efforts were bound to fall short. The indictment seemed accurate enough, but I didn't intend to rock the boat. I gave lip service to catalog identifications and carved out my own courses. I was allowed to do so. An unwritten Principle of Tolerance operated for senior faculty, giving them the right to form their own circle of coherence out of the curricular muddle. That meant we aimed for a state of being—tenured, all promotions safely behind us—in which we could reduce our obligations to an academic design, to a mere formality.

The strikers meant to end this hypocrisy. They intended to impose unity by force. That's one consequence I saw to the call for relevance. Logic and coherence could be achieved only by dissolving the vested interests of the separate departments. That would take a revolution.

The members of the Establishment—and that included God knows who, perhaps me—were denounced as racist, fascist oppressors, as slave masters. The BSU language didn't invite negotiation. It was a call to arms, intended not only for college sympathizers, but for off-campus Blacks.

Despite their brilliant sensitivity to the nature of violence, despite their unsentimental hard view of power, the desire of the strikers for a definitive confrontation that would employ fist, gun, bomb, made me feel that they, too, were affected by our cowboy myths.

Could I personally accept the implications of the BSU demands? They sometimes seemed to be a threat to all academic value. What would happen to Ph.D. scholarship? Overboard. What of the dream to transform our college into another Berkeley? Forget it. Those years spent mastering ancient and medieval studies? Out the window. Metaphysics and *Beowulf?* Chaucer and the Stuart and Tudor geneologies? Duns Scotus? St. Thomas? Aristotle? Shakespeare? Your ordinary Ph.D. would have to sacrifice his entire investment. And why? Weren't we the least guilty of all Americans of acts of violence against Blacks?

Hayakawa, when he was still a professor of English, spoke for many of the faculty in rejecting the charge of racism. "If the word 'racist' is applied to S.F. State College, what word is there for Rhodesia?"

I wasn't impressed by his reservations. Nor could I sympathize with the fear that academic standards might be lowered, when I myself doubted those standards. My opposition to the BSU stemmed from my unwillingness to endanger this safe harbor. The Blacks threatened to shake us loose from our anchorage. They came on like a gang of baddies, quite aware of their effect—indeed, soliciting it with their language and rehearsed bearing and their shades and berets and leather jackets—telling us what a cowboy country this was and yet coming on like cowboys themselves. Did they imagine we were the villains? Did they really see us as "pigs"? Did they see themselves as knights who were prepared to die for their community and a Black Studies Program? Or was the violence a mere bluff, a tactic meant to galvanize a community that generally talked around its problems without making heroic efforts to solve them? What were the real sentiments behind the bristling mixture of street idiom and Maoist jargon? One thing most white faculty were agreed upon—the word "pig" was in itself an act of violence.

The destiny of pigs is not an enviable one. I can understand why anyone can be made nervous by the designation. A Godard movie called *Weekend* played at a local theater during the strike and was popular with students. It is a movie that is brimful of slaughter. Cadavers dangle from wrecked autos like exotic fruit. But I found the deaths merely a case of Mercurochrome and ketchup. I was under no illusion that any person died to make this movie. But a non-person died. A butcher slams a fat pig in the back of the head with a mallet. His forefeet cave in. Then the butcher wrenches the massive head to the side, jabs a knife into the throat, and real gore pumps into view. A real death spasm follows. You can't really do in a man, even when the script calls for it. But pigs exist in order to be slaughtered. Call a man a pig and you've prepared him for a terrible destiny. Words are at times more dreadful than sticks and stones. The sticks and stones won't be used until the name is used.

Who knows that better than the black man who is very careful about the designation of things? He is especially careful about the designation which he will accept for himself. He knows what his destiny has been when others have been free to name him.

The words the BSU chose to report its demands indicated a hostility powerful enough to rock the boat. "Racist pig!" "Fascist!" "Slavemaster!"

Did they, for instance, mean me? That first week of the strike was bewildering. I struggled with the contradiction of its violent inception and its noble sentiments. The Blacks made the same charges I did about academic hypocrisies. They meant to solve the contradictions even if they had to overturn the boat.

I wanted to talk things over and find out whether we could agree on common objectives after our feelings had been vented. I had been reconciled to alien people by attending a funeral. Couldn't we end hostility by means of a nonviolent encounter? I was afraid of what might happen if we remained "pigs" to each other. Many cops—as the Blacks knew well—considered long-hairs and Blacks to be "animals." The forces of law and order were free—just as the butcher of *Weekend* was free—to bludgeon "animals."

I wanted a public confrontation between all the parties involved so that we could discard the dangerous notion that we were "pigs."

What was so frustrating in the first days of the strike was the reluctance of the college administration to provide information to the academic community. President Smith's policy was to keep the plant operating with as little acknowledgment of crisis as possible. I suppose he hoped the strike would lose its energy and the campus return to normal operation. Maybe there was a reason for this. The scope of the strike wasn't defined at first. It was possible that the BSU and their cohorts improvised the strike from day to day. Any response which prematurely fixed positions might have strengthened a waning effort. The administration evidently decided that it was best to say little and to say that little as murkily as possible. President Smith was under great pressure from the governor and the trustees to resolve the crisis with brutally simple measures. Governor Reagan was impatient with what he regarded as dilatory and craven tactics. He saw the problem as one for the police. He offered unlimited police and military power to Smith. Smith tried to occupy a middle ground but he was assailed from both sides. However well-intentioned, his policy was manipulative. It didn't allow the faculty an active part in dealing with the crisis. The students were scornful of his obfuscating rhetoric. To a generation that wanted to come to new terms with language, the best policy was to speak one's mind at the height of feeling and let the chips fall where they may.

In retrospect, I see that my own hunger for clarity was naïve. I wanted answers, when I really needed experience. I had to be educated about complicated persons and deep issues, and it was an education that wouldn't allow me to be a spectator. What commenced on November 6, triggered by the black demands, was a far more elaborate process than merely determining the merits of the case. Our academic life was at stake. To say that the education was dialectical is merely to suggest the constant tension as many of us oscillated from one extreme to the other, from sympathy for the revolution to sympathy for the repression. Only at the extremes was there any serenity of conviction.

I found relief in action, but the relief was only temporary. Actions were only speciously definitive. The old confusions swarmed back in their aftermath. I imagined that the initial violence would enable me to assume unequivocal attitudes toward the BSU. It didn't. The damage seen in retrospect was not very serious. It produced strong reactions in a community not subject to the kind of intimidation generally confined to ghettos. We were suddenly made aware that we were powerless to command obedience when there was no will to obey. With the violation of our corridors, and classes, and commons—the space we had simply accepted as *ours*—we recognized the peril of our impotence. We had always been impotent.

Perhaps I didn't want information but only reassurance that everything could be restored to normal. Perhaps I hoped that we might dull the edge of revolutionary talk. But the boat rocked and rocked and no amount of talking could bring it to rest.

7 · stalling for time?

LEO LITWAK

A week after the strike began, President Smith finally called a faculty assembly, and for two weeks we talked. I now see that hope for a consensus was absurd. I had only to glance over the approximately seven hundred faculty in the Main Auditorium to see that we had no common appearance, little common interest, and not much basis for a common will. Without parliamentary rules to regulate even our trivial transactions we couldn't maintain the façade of a community.

What did a professor of accounting have in common with a professor of philosophy? His rank and his pay schedule. What else? Status in the eyes of the community? The same question could be asked of a variety of other disciplines. We were not one faculty but a congeries of faculties.

There were other differences besides discipline, of course —age being an obvious one. You only had to check appearances to see that we were a variety of generations. A row of middle-aged professors from the Business School wore the uniform of the fifties—three-button suit, regimental stripe tie, horn-rimmed spectacles, hair trimmed short, clean shaven. At the other extreme were junior members of the humanities—granny glasses, tie-dyed shirts, bell-bottom jeans, high boots, flourishing manes and beards and mustaches.

The college had in its time gone through radical metamorphoses, changing from a normal school in the forties to a "swinging" community school in the fifties, then in the sixties to an institution on the prowl for academic respectability. Each era contributed a different faculty. The heterogeneity was manifest in dress, language, and vested interest. It was a colorful mixture in peacetime, but chaos in war.

Still, the majority of faculty were anti-boat-rockers, willing to accept a Black Studies Program if it could be accommodated to the status quo. However, the majority of faculty also feared that the fifteen demands were just the preview of an insatiable revolutionary appetite. They accepted the necessity of a police presence. Some who felt committed to a liberal stand had misgivings about the police, but the violent student tactics clarified matters for them. They denounced the strikers as "fascists" and supported a tough stand against appeasement.

On the other hand, a sizable minority of the faculty wanted the college to settle its own affairs without calling in the police, even if that meant putting aside ordinary classroom business for a semester-long convocation.

Smith took the middle ground, insisting that we act in terms of what was possible. We were hemmed in by a fiscal crisis which he attributed in part to an angry public, unwilling to vote for bond issues; in part to a hostile legislature, dominated by Reagan; in part to an unsympathetic board of trustees. Smith saw the obstacles to militant action but he proposed no alternatives. Perhaps there were none.

Smith's tenure was a bad time for the middle ground. He stood in the path of a confrontation that was bound to occur, expressing as it did the powerful antipathies that divided the college and the nation.

The first day of the faculty assembly, November 12, produced nothing more than a recommendation to the chancellor that George Murray's job be restored until due process could operate. Then, presumably, he could be dismissed with propriety.

The ad hoc committee, scorning such piddling results, declared itself on strike. The next morning, three dozen faculty paraded at the main entrance of the campus, bearing picket signs. It wasn't clear—other than their declaration that it was so—that they were on strike, since many faculty had already withdrawn their classes from campus, and not necessarily out of sympathy for the strikers. Some felt intimidated by possible violence. Others responded to the fears and sympathies that divided their own students and preferred a more neutral climate for classwork.

The faculty meeting resumed on November 13 despite the opposition of those who believed that it was a waste of time and, even worse, a surrender to the strikers. Indeed, after a morning of tiresome debate it looked as if nothing would be accomplished and it was doubtful that a quorum could be summoned for the afternoon session. It took less than two days to discover how impotent we were.

It was at this point that the Tactical Squad intervened. Suddenly, the police marched on campus during the noon hour, when the commons were most densely occupied. They went directly to the vicinity of the BSU hut.

Afterward, a police spokesman said that they had responded to a false alarm. Yet there they were, in the midst of a crowd that was committed to a violent reaction should police come on campus. And here were the *ultimate police.* A crowd swarmed around them. Hemmed in by the taunting, pressing students, the police started to swing. They hit everyone around them. Food trays sailed through the air. The police were pelted by clods of turf. They pulled out their pistols. Students screamed and fled. A BSU leader was clubbed down. I saw two Tac Squad officers haul a captive Black across the commons, trailed by several hundred students. The black man, his arms wrenched behind him, urged the crowd to stay back. One officer extended his pistol at arm's length and wheeled about to ward off the crowd. The students withdrew like grass before a scythe as the pistol came around.

We were on a most peculiar battlefield. Around us were the landmarks of a secure and serene life—the library, the dining room, the classrooms, the gymnasium, the auditorium. The police weren't fighting thugs, but young men and women, some of them our finest students. What kind of a war was this? The sight of pistols and gas masks was incredible. (That was only my first reaction, however. Before the month was out, I could only see the place as a battlefield. Its other function seemed peculiar. And when it was all over, months later, and I could again safely walk the commons, I felt as a veteran might on revisiting some Normandy beach.)

Some of the Tac Squad had difficulty disengaging themselves from the students who were trying to encircle them. Riot sticks thrust out, the police moved back step by step toward a paddy wagon behind them. Someone informed the ad hoc committee, picketing at the main entrance, and the professors, still carrying their picket signs, marched to the scene and put themselves between the police and the students. The students allowed themselves to be restrained.

Then a stone was lofted from the crowd. The retreating cops paused. A sergeant stepped forward. A professor begged him, "Don't do it." The sergeant politely but firmly moved the professor aside and stepped into the mob, which parted for him. He collared the presumed stone thrower. He batted him down with his right stick, then dragged him back to the police line, which resumed its nicely choreographed withdrawal. The clubbed boy, clutching his head, was dragged to the paddy wagon, which absorbed the police and their prisoner. The students then turned on the professors. A leader of the Progressive Labor Party, obviously distraught by the tension, invited the crowd to observe the obscene role that faculty played, aborting revolutionary action, serving the Establishment after voicing radical sentiments.

I myself found something foolish about professors who imagined that their presence by itself could bring sanity to the battlefield. This was to presume oneself removed by rank and station from any danger of assault. Didn't professors know that they could bleed, too, that police were not awed by academic status?

Immediately following the riotous scene, the faculty assembly resumed. A quorum was barely marshaled. Action became decisive and dramatic. The rules were changed to allow motions to become immediately effective, without waiting for a canvass of the entire faculty. A motion to suspend all academic business in favor of a continuing faculty meeting was overwhelmingly passed. In order to meet the contractual obligations that the trustees had warned would be enforced, the meeting was proposed as an educational program in lieu of scheduled classes. The motion wouldn't have had a chance if the threat of the Tac Squad's arrival on campus weren't so real.

President Smith reluctantly ordered the campus closed in order to prevent further violence. He announced that he would keep it shut until the situation was under control.

Governor Reagan called the order that closed the campus "unprecedented." Assembly minority leader Jess Unruh demanded that the governor restore the campus to full use.

The faculty operated in its next meeting with what the local newspapers called "rare speed." There was an appearance of united action, but in fact, only a minority of the faculty participated.

One resolution "respectfully" requested Dumke to rescind the suspension of George Murray. Another asked for the implementation of a Black Studies Program by the following semester. A task force was created to consider the establishment of a comprehensive Ethnic Studies Program. The fifteen demands seemed close to realization. (This was an illusion. The faculty was to pass almost seventy resolutions and not one was ever implemented. The faculty voice had no audience in Sacramento and that's where the power was.)

Professor Hayakawa addressed the faculty in a prepared speech on November 15. "What my colleagues seem to be forgetting is that we not only owe a lot to black Americans and to the fulfillment of just expectations. We also have a standing obligation to the 17,500 or more students—white, black, yellow, red, and brown—who are not on strike and have every right to expect continuation of their education." He demanded that the campus be open to instruction. "The big problem is how to get classes going again in spite of threats and disruptions . . . we must permit no one to disrupt or dismiss our classes. No one—no matter how great his need to establish his black consciousness—has the right to break into my classes and tell my students that they are dismissed." He called for a joint student faculty peace force. He called for a "resolution of support authorizing Dr. Smith to suspend students found creating disorder and to get court orders when necessary to keep disruptive students and non-students off the campus." His speech was loudly applauded. In the course of it he said that he was speaking "on behalf of the silent majority of Negro students advancing themselves and their race without recourse to violence and intimidation . . . they want to be treated as responsible human beings and as equals in moral terms as well as in terms of economic and educational opportunity."

It was the first time I'd heard Hayakawa. I understood his anger, which corresponded to my own impulse when I first heard of student violence. Yet it surprised me that nothing of the subtlety of the issues had occured to him, that he had managed to preserve his initial anger and simplicity. It gave him a certain power. A majority of the faculty were of like mind. Yet how foolhardy, how remarkably arrogant—how nervy, too—after seeing the display of black rage and the complexity of black allegiances, to imply that he, Hayakawa, spoke for the silent majority of Blacks. It became abundantly clear, a few weeks later, that Hayakawa did not speak naïvely or heedlessly. He was prepared to accept all the implications of a hard-nosed stand. He understood even more clearly than we did—and most of us were aware of our unpopularity—where power lay and what would be the outcome of its firm exercise.

Once again the public power announced its opposition to closing the campus. Reagan termed the campus shutdown "unnecessary" since "ample law enforcement support was available to keep the campus open." He made it clear to President Smith that school had better reopen on Tuesday, November 19, despite the faculty resolutions, and that police power be used unsparingly.

Reagan said, "By capitulating to a small group of faculty and student troublemakers, the S.F. State College administration showed a woeful lack of understanding of divisive tactics which were used to disrupt the campus." He attributed the disruption to a mere eighty to one hundred "hard-core militant agitators." On Monday, November 28, Smith was summoned to Los Angeles to attend an emergency trustee's meeting. He was accompanied by the entire S.F. State Academic Senate. At that meeting he was given a directive ordering the immediate resumption of classes. The trustees further stipulated that there would be "no negotiations, arbitration, or concessions of student grievances or

complaints except through the ordinary channels of communication and decision-making at the college." They directed that negotiations could take place "only after order
has been restored and the educational process resumed."
They ordered disciplinary action against any student or
faculty member who attempted to disrupt the campus. The
only Negro trustee, Edward Lee, described the resolution as
"a rigid position that will not let us consider the causes of the
trouble on campus. Maybe the trouble is that students have
tried to get action through normal channels and have failed."

Smith announced that the campus would be reopened the
following day. He summonned a general faculty meeting to
tell us of the trustees' decision. Meanwhile, he suggested that
each department meet separately with its faculty and students to consider means of reducing tension so that instruction might resume in an orderly fashion.

The senate members who accompanied Smith to the
trustees' meeting reported to the faculty. They were generally bitter at the scant courtesy offered to the faculty representatives. As one senator put it, "They made me feel as if I
were a little boy in short pants caught with my hand in the
cookie jar."

The trustees questioned Smith on the substance of the
Black Studies Program, even though the ground had been
covered again and again.

Were they being asked to practice "reverse racism" by
establishing a program taught by and for Blacks exclusively?
What about the demand for total departmental autonomy?
What check would there be on hiring practices if the department had sole responsibility? Was it possible that a Black
Studies Program might become a haven for such firebrands
as Eldridge Cleaver and George Murray? What if the curriculum openly sponsored revolution? Would the trustees be

in the position of providing footholds for Black Panthers and
Maoists?

There were no funds available, Smith was told.

A black member of the Academic Senate bitterly denounced the trustees' meeting as racist. He observed that
while the trustees protested the blackness of the Black Studies Department, they accepted with equanimity the white-
ness of their own board, which had a single Negro member,
and the all-whiteness of most college departments throughout the state. The trustees were alarmed by the demand that
all black applicants be admitted to the college by the fall of
1969. But were they alarmed by the inadequate representation of the black community on the campus?

Another senator offered his opinion that the trustees considered the campus to be a factory, with professors as re-
placeable components of the assembly line. To them, the real
heart of the college was the committee room, not the classroom. After all, the state system employed thousands of
faculty, but there were only twenty-two trustees.

Again the chord of unity was struck. Disrespect by the
trustees was our common grievance. In fact, the chancellor
dealt with us as if we were absent-minded professors, or
gullible children, or a colony not yet prepared for home rule.

The faculty, in a rebellious mood, refused to extend a vote
of confidence to President Smith. Instead, they passed a resolution stopping all formal business in favor of a campus-wide
convocation. The students cheered the news.

Smith's policy of riding out the trouble by continuing business as usual hadn't worked. He agreed to meet a large group
of faculty who wanted to argue for his support of a convocation. He met us in the library—one of the few times in the
past two weeks he had been able to leave the barricaded
Administration Building.

He confessed that he was under enormous pressure to take a harder line and that our intransigence hadn't helped him a bit. We had deprived him of room to maneuver. A faculty member interrupted Smith and urged him to stand with us rather than with the administration. "We are your constituency." Smith answered that he represented many interests, not only those who wanted a convocation. He also had an obligation to those who wanted to teach and who perhaps were in the majority. Wilner mentioned the danger of continued conflict between police and students. Was it worth keeping the campus open if someone were killed? Others also urged Smith to reconsider his opposition to suspending formal instruction. Bloodshed was unavoidable if he accepted the trustees' command. Shouldn't there be another way?

Smith surrendered. "All right. Let's do it." And we cheered him.

So in defiance of the trustees, President Smith summoned a college-wide convocation to replace scheduled instruction.

The coalition of Third World and BSU agreed to the convocation on the condition that all classes be suspended. They were determined to maintain the pressure of a strike. They feared that a convocation might degenerate into talk and the strike lose its momentum. It was rumored that the moderate leadership of the BSU had barely prevailed over those who opposed the convocation for just that reason.

The convocation began Wednesday, November 20. The faculty assembled in the Main Auditorium. Closed-circuit television carried the proceedings to other parts of the campus. All TV networks had crews present. On stage in the Main Auditorium, facing a bank of cameras in the orchestra pit, was the academic contingent on the right, the TWLF representatives on the left. They were immediately identifiable by dress. On the right were tweed and serge and subdued ties and Oxford shoes. On the left were field jackets, red scarves, sunglasses, leather jackets, berets, boots. A bereted BSU leader almost immediately set the tone. Pointing to Smith he asked, "When is this man gonna get off his fat ass?"

A new language, studded with "bullshit" and "pig" and "motherfucker," was turned loose on campus. It was a bullying performance that made the juices run.

The administration representatives remained calm. They shuffled papers. Smith puffed a cigar. He didn't appear to take offense at the abuse. The administration made reference to faculty allocations relative to enrollments, state codes, salary schedules. They couldn't keep an audience with language like that. They responded to revolutionary diction with a bureaucratic jargon.

Yet, President Smith could move me when he showed himself hurt by the insults. "I know what you're trying to do," he said to a black administrator who criticized his failure to communicate with the dissident students. "You're trying to isolate me from the students and the faculty. I've been driven to the edge so many times that I have become ineffective." He won my sympathy by admitting to a confusion that we all experienced. Then he proceeded to waste it with a tone that was as dry as dust and a syntax that seemed deliberately obfuscatory, as though he wanted to stifle any passion which could have led him to an extreme reaction.

When the strike leaders discovered that some classes were being held as scheduled, they refused to continue participating in the convocation. After a two-day interruption, Smith yielded once more. All classes were suspended.

The convocation resumed, but the administration representatives waited on stage for an hour. When the strike representatives finally arrived, they were led by a more belligerent voice, Jerry Varnado, a BSU official who wasn't about to be reconciled by sweet reason. A burly man with a mustache, wearing a sweater and sunglasses, his first move was to wave disparagingly at Smith and say, "This pig, Robert Smith . . ." He unleashed a chorus of boos. Varnado stared at the one thousand assembled faculty and told us disdainfully, "We aren't reasonable. We are madmen. We are terrorists for the sake of our freedom." What had a reasonable policy gained black people? Nothing, said Varnado, but interminable "bullshit."

He pulled out his *Little Red Book* and raised it for all to see, and quoted Chairman Mao: "Whoever sides with the revolutionary people in words alone but acts otherwise is a revolutionary in speech. Whoever sides with the revolutionary people in deed as well as word is a revolutionary in the full sense."

He read again the ten demands of the BSU. These demands weren't negotiable. They weren't requests. They were demands. The BSU wasn't playing games, offering ten demands in the hope that five would be accepted. These ten demands reflected their *minimum* needs. They could have listed eighty demands if they wanted to negotiate, but they only listed ten. It was true that these demands were only the beginning. "We haven't asked for our freedom yet."

What so depressed those of us who occupied the middle ground (the middle swamp would be a better image) was that there was no desire for negotiation on either side. The demands might simply be the prelude to revolution and few of us had come so far as to want that.

A statement attributed to the BSU, issued December 2, seemed to confirm this suspicion:

We started a strike. We will end up in a revolution. The revolution of our generation of our time, for our people, for survival and a humane and just world.

One without racist pigs. One without racist administrators. One without prisons packed with black souls, ghettos smothered in poverty and rats and roaches, schools producing illiterates and addicts and humanoids.

In order for such a world to be, a revolution must occur. Complete and total change. All traces of the exploitation, greed, racism, supremacist insanity have to be destroyed.

We are starting with the educational system in the State of California of this racist country. The educational system which leads millions of minds to the slaughterhouse every year.

Throughout our struggle, our actions, our tactics will define to the black community our sincerity and intent, as well as expose the contradiction of education for the trustees and politicians.

Our support increases. Our struggle escalates.

Our oppressors move against us. Our struggle escalates.

Our leaders are jailed, assassinated, exiled. Our struggle escalates.

We move into the community. Our struggle escalates.

Innocent people are brutalized. Our struggle escalates.

ACTION, ESCALATION, REACTION, ESCALATION.

The power to escalate comes from the action of the people and the reaction of the power structure. Action-activists. Reaction-reactionaries. Escalation-revolution.

We have already gone from striking to disrupting to closing the school down.

Whatever activity we engage in, we must be able to sustain it. As Brother Stokely said, the struggle has to be sustained; if it's only one picket sign . . . it stays.

We must continue to disrupt for the purpose of closing this racist institution down permanently. No classrooms, no offices, no order, no academic façade, nothing is exempt from disruption.

In one sense, the Blacks had far more invested in the struggle than we did. But in another, they had less. What did we have at stake? Merely our jobs, our careers, our homes, our cars, our rank and status. They struggled in behalf of their community. They felt responsibility for "black souls in prison," for "ghettos smothered in poverty and rats and roaches," for "schools producing illiterates, addicts and humanoids." They wanted revolution. San Francisco State was only a step on the way. The battle for the college was a skirmish to them. Its loss would perhaps be worth sustaining if the struggle were escalated in the country at large. And that's why we had more invested. For those of us whose world was defined by the campus, the loss of the college didn't represent a step toward a new future, but into an abyss.

When later the Blacks cursed us for worrying about the loss of our paychecks, reminding us of the ghetto poverty they were determined to halt, I felt guilty that my concern was so selfish, that I couldn't share the utopian idealism which prepared them for sacrifice. In my more resentful moments, I felt that their sacrifice wasn't all that much. They had everything to gain, but what had they to lose? Their chains? The revolution was their vocation. They could practice it anywhere.

The strong language reflected the official BSU line, but many of the leaders, speaking to small faculty groups, were more conciliatory. There was a difference between public and private posture. You listened to a man address the multitudes and his tone was chilling. Privately, you might find him subtler, gentler, thoughtful about tactics and objectives and concerned for the college. It was a relief to turn from the unyielding public stance to the rumor of a more moderate policy. We were reassured by a professor intimate with Third World leaders that despite public rhetoric, the strikers were not revolutionary and that we shouldn't interpret too literally their refusal to negotiate.

Still the public stance was a commitment that was hard to shake, and it must have made the convocation a very tricky maneuver for the strike leaders whose rank and file were suspicious of talk. They feared the convocation would drain energy from their strike. For some at least, it must have been a relief to have the convocation ended and the battle resumed.

When Smith was again called to Los Angeles by the trustees and presented with conditions for maintaining an open campus which he found unacceptable, he offered his resignation. It was immediately accepted. Smith had been neither an effective agent of state policy, nor had he the power or inclination to satisfy student demands, so he was bound to go. The college received the announcement of his resignation in the late afternoon and shortly thereafter the name of his successor, Professor Hayakawa. Reagan said, "I think we have found our man. I'm delighted with the selection."

We had hoped that Smith would quit his post in such a way as to rally the faculty. Presumably he might have unified us by damning the outrageous interference with his office by the state. But he resigned quietly. He made no incendiary statement. He didn't call for resistance to trustee rule. And why should he have? He opposed the strike. He didn't want to arouse faculty support for a radical cause. So he tiptoed off stage without making a stir, and sacrificed what little voice he had, by his unobtrusive exit. And we were left leaderless.

The convocation was doomed. The radical analysis was correct that negotiations were impossible because no one at the college had the power to meet the student demands. The only service the convocation could perform for the strike was possibly to recruit students and faculty to its ranks. But the BSU didn't overestimate this service. As Professor Juan Martinez of the TWLF expressed it, "The purpose of the convocation is to co-opt the movement and to stall for time." A BSU leader denounced the convocation: "I challenge this whole meeting. Blacks agreed we'd strike until demands were met. People are still meeting classes. Our first priority is to build a strike." Another expressed his despair and anger: "We are contained in this small room while the world outside continues as usual. It's a vast contradiction." He meant that the continued parlaying was a contradiction to the militant spirit.

The strikers believed that force, not negotiation, would bring about the equitable reordering of power. The BSU's argument for the strike was that established interest would never voluntarily surrender its power.

Reagan, reflecting public sentiment, announced a similar disbelief in negotiation. He urged a policy of massive police intervention to quickly blunt the revolutionary thrust.

The ad hoc committee called a meeting to consider the emergency, and perhaps two hundred faculty attended. But the powerful energy released by Smith's resignation had no direction. We shared a common grievance but we lacked an organization to express it. It was a chaotic moment. Students waited for faculty leadership and expressed outrage at our continued confusion. We shouted at each other. Motions were jumbled, parliamentarians quarreled. The announcement made at that point, of Hayakawa's elevation to office, was a huge relief. It was greeted with a roar of laughter. Faculty laughed, Blacks laughed, SDS people laughed. The posture of belligerence was relaxed. The choice of Hayakawa seemed comically appropriate, as though it were the *reductio ad absurdum* of the Establishment position.

The night of Hayakawa's appointment—November 26—
the ad hoc committee called another meeting at the Gallery
Lounge to press the advantage of our sudden unity. I arrived
late, expecting to find the high spirits of the afternoon still
prevailing. But it was a totally different assembly. The mood
was depressed. The ad hoc committee had neither the authority nor the organization to pull together a heterogeneous
faculty. So long as the committee remained a small group of
like minds it could act in concert. But it couldn't rally a group
as ideologically varied as was assembled that night in the
Gallery Lounge. It had to improvise an organization. Volunteers were urged to sign up for committee work. There was
a publicity committee, a state college liaison committee, a
community liaison committee, a student liaison committee,
a finance committee. The faculty milled around in the center
of the room, some edging toward the door as the rhetoric
became more desperate. Few volunteers stepped forward.
Many of the student leaders were present and they appeared
stunned by our disunity, as if they hadn't really believed their
own indictment of us.

Hayakawa's appointment made real what we had privately
thought were paranoid fears of Reagan's intentions.
Hayakawa had preached the hardest of all lines. He was on
record as favoring extreme measures to be rid of troublemak-
ing faculty and students. We had no doubt as to what would
follow. Cowboys of all persuasions wanted a bloody confrontation. Some had their own plausible justifications for bloody
violence as an education and an initiation. I could sometimes
understand and sympathize with this point of view. But in
the three weeks following Hayakawa's appointment, I lost all
heart for it. I couldn't take a long view. I couldn't subscribe
to an education purchased at either end of a riot stick. The
police, too, would be educated. They would learn to club the

kind of people they had never hit before.

That night, as one by one we sneaked from the Gallery Lounge, a firebrand physical science instructor shook his fists at us and shouted, "Have you no honor?" He addressed the students, who were as glum as we were, "You see—fifteen years in the same job, a family, a house—oh, hell!" He gave up in histrionic despair.

When all unity seemed to have disappeared, Gary Hawkins, president of the local A.F.T., finally stepped forward. "Okay, I've tried to keep the union out of this. Now there's no alternative." He called a meeting of the executive council for the following day.

So the union entered the fray which it had avoided since the membership had criticized the letter of November 5, supporting the BSU strike. No other faculty organization had a method for defying the authority of management.

A pattern of confrontation developed during the weeks preceding the Christmas vacation. At noon each day, striking students assembled at the speaker's platform in defiance of Hayakawa's edict. Police massed in streets near the campus, gathered from law enforcement agencies throughout the Bay Area. There were gold-helmeted state troopers, blue-helmeted city police, white-helmeted deputy sheriffs, some with full visors, others with half visors, some with long riot sticks, others with short chubby billies, all equipped with gas masks, pistols, and mace. Within two days, six hundred police were massed on campus. The newcomers to riot duty appeared tense and gloomy. The old-timers joked with passing students. "If I come back once more," said a member of the Tac Squad, "I'll get a degree."

The strike leaders warmed up the crowd. Fists pumped the air; there was a chant of "ON STRIKE." There were, by this time, almost three thousand students involved. Specta-

tors ringed the entire commons. Only those close to the platform were able to hear, since the speakers were confined to
the use of bull horns. The police remained out of sight until
the demonstrators moved in the direction of the classroom
buildings. It was primarily a white crowd, some in Levi's,
some wearing army field jackets, a few with helmets. Some
had long hair and beards. Others were shorn. The exotic and
the pedestrian mingled. As the demonstrators approached
Hayakawa's office, they chanted obscenities. It was a
steamed-up, exuberant crowd. A helicopter circled above,
tracing their movements. Television cameras caught the action from rooftops. A line of police closed off the Business and
Social Science Building, legs spread wide, riot sticks gripped
at both ends. Troopers marched in from the parking lot and
closed off one side of the commons. They wore leather
gloves; the riot sticks were tied to thongs wrapped around
their hands. A police photographer accompanied each squad.
Some units were equipped with pepper fog, a device that
looked as if it had been lifted from a Buck Rogers serial. From
the loudspeakers on the roof of the Administration Building,
we heard Hayakawa's voice. "Bystanders and curiosity seek-
ers, please leave. Please leave. This is a warning. This is a
warning. Watch these events on evening television. This is an
illegal assembly. Go to your classes. Go to the library. Walk
away from the police. Do not get close to the police." Later
his voice became more urgent. "Innocent bystanders, please
leave. There comes a time when there are no innocent bystanders and that is the time when the very size of a crowd
constitutes a threat. For your own protection, please leave."
The "please" was stressed as if to say, "Leave for your own
good. I beg of you. I don't want to see you hurt." But the tone
was also angry. "If you want trouble, stay there. The police
will see that you get it." How could he still be angry after

seeing the punishment these troublemakers received?

The police swept forward with threatening motions of their clubs. They divided the crowd, moved it from the center of the commons. The action suddenly became vicious. Police picked out a striker; riot sticks flailed. They brought him down. Sometimes they continued swinging when he was prone. The victim was forced to his belly, his hands bound behind him. A riot stick pressed his throat like a vise. He was jerked up, his head stretched to the side, his arms twisted in back, sometimes bloody from head wounds. I was told by several who had been arrested that that was only the beginning of the ordeal. What happened in the police vans was something else. One hundred twenty-five arrests were made in two weeks. One morning the police pursued students who had thrown rocks into the commons dining room. They locked the doors and then, according to students who had been eating breakfast, they lashed out indiscriminately. These actions were viewed by thousands. And the ranks of demonstrators were increased. Each day police helicopters circled above the commons, directing the forces below. Each day the students assembled before the speaker's platform. And they marched toward the classroom buildings. The police formations closed them off. The police dispersed them. Police were struck by flying objects. One was seriously hurt by a thrown brick. Students were bloodied by flailing night sticks. Hayakawa viewed the action from his office window. Perhaps from that perspective the encounter was merely spectacle, with dramatic movements by uniformed officers, great sweeps that overwhelmed the ominous hordes of students. There was something spectacular in these scenes on our commons. Lovely days, marvelous costumes, students chanting, "ON STRIKE, ON STRIKE, SHUT IT DOWN, SHUT IT DOWN," then screaming at the approach of a skirmish line. The action was for one moment clotted, then flailing night sticks, a pell-mell exodus from the center as though the demonstrators were magnetic filings, repelled by a negative pole beneath the center of the commons. "There's good excitement and bad excitement," Hayakawa had said to incredulous reporters after one such scene, admitting that his excitement might not be good.

The general sentiment of students and faculty nonetheless favored a negotiated settlement. The BSU claimed to be unwilling. But it became apparent that the governor was every bit as intransigent.

"There's nothing to settle," Reagan told newsmen in answer to the question whether he believed progress could be made toward a settlement during the Christmas holidays. Hayakawa was doing a fine job. What remained was a police problem. For two weeks there were bloody confrontations. Just before Christmas vacation, leaders of the black community appeared on campus and attempted to divert the students from open conflict with police. They tried to route a student march away from the Administration Building, toward a ceremonial circling of the campus. But some of the BSU leaders didn't want the conflict eased. One of them took over the crowd. He led it toward Hayakawa's office and up the steps. They were met by Tac Squad officers with drawn pistols. The leader yelled, "Is there anyone real bad who'll follow me?" When no one responded, the attack turned against the Business Building. Students with two-by-fours smashed windows. That brought another sweep of cops and more bloody heads.

I couldn't understand how the students experiencing the violence were able to return for more punishment. Perhaps the observer is more terrified than the participant. Perhaps, once involved in action, you don't feel the blows, don't experience the terror, and are purged of guilt and anxiety.

But the daily confrontation, staged at a regular place, at a regular time, noted by reporters, recorded by sound and camera men, suddenly seemed like a bloody game. The police maneuvers, far from being restrained, impressed me as cruel. Why didn't the police simply make arrests and let the courts decide the issue? Instead, they played a childish game of tag which inevitably had an outcome in a sadistic release of antipathies. At least in combat I had no choice. I had to stay on the battlefield. I didn't have to stay here. I decided to leave. However, I felt the need to clarify ambiguities and I again returned.

In retrospect, I see no way of having foreshortened the game. Each side had to develop its own capabilities through battlefield testing. Police had undertaken something unusual that needed getting used to. They were clobbering the heads of young men and women who were not criminals. Perhaps when they discovered the enormous popularity of their action were they free to cut loose.

After the failure of the convocation, I began to realize that I wouldn't get off the hook by someone's lucid revelation of the causes of the strike. Nor was anyone going to be able to reassure me that some course of action would bring a happy solution. Talking was useless. The established interest wouldn't allow talk to change anything. The strikers, on the other hand, feared losing the momentum of their strike if they stopped to talk. My ambiguities remained unclarified. And there was no time left to hunt for options.

S. I. Hayakawa
Excerpts from public statement
November 30, 1968

I understand and respect the Negro demand for self-determination and the right to make his own decision. But self-
determination is not given, it is earned. Self-determination
comes from having enough money to be your own boss, or
from having enough intelligence and creativity so that others
are willing to entrust great projects on you. Let me tell the
members of the BSU that I am on their side. I want to be
counted as an ally.

I think we can look forward to Monday with hope and
anticipation. After weeks of hearing from angry dissidents
and assorted fanatics, we have finally come to the stage
where the voice of the quiet and thoughtful majority is being
heard, loud and clear. The Faculty Renaissance, representing the attitude of the large majority of our professors, has
come out in support of our continued functioning as an academic institution. The Committee for an Academic Environment, representing the views of an overwhelming majority
of our students, has organized itself into a welcoming committee for our return to campus.

On Monday morning the Committee for an Academic Environment and a group of Japanese-American students will
greet everyone with a blue arm band to wear. This arm band
is to symbolize support for the following:
1. Racial equality
2. Social justice
3. Nonviolence
4. The resumption of education

To those in my audience who are students or staff members, or members of the faculty at San Francisco State Col-

lege, I ask you to take these arm bands and wear them. What we have to gain is the restoration of the free and exciting atmosphere of intellectual, cultural, political, and sartorial diversity that has always characterized San Francisco. What we have to lose is the college itself.

8 · joining up

HERBERT WILNER

The American Federation of Teachers, Local 1352, was established at S.F. State in 1959. I witnessed this beginning, I knew its faculty organizers, but I didn't join. In the ensuing years, the union's modestly increasing membership came to include some of my closest friends, and still I didn't join. Many of my reservations were more a matter of temperament than reason. If I considered myself above what I detested in the *academic,* I also thought myself to be apart from *union* and *local.* If I had little that was humanly in common with academics, I also had little, by way of the work itself, in common with laborers. But the union rhetoric on our campus over the years paid little attention to such temperamental distinctions. There was, for me, too much partisan crankiness in it, too much of that sour inclination to find fault everywhere in order that the union cause might thrive somewhere. The style bored me; sometimes it embarrassed me. But on December 4, 1968, I joined the A.F.T., Local 1352. I ran to it. By that day almost every untested and self-protecting assumption I had lived with in twenty years of college teaching had been shredded.

Primarily, terrifyingly, there was the violence already committed and the unpredictable violence, which could be even worse, possibly before us. Serious injury was unavoidable. Death was possible. It could come from anywhere, be delivered by anyone. The mutinous flood of passion spilling out of students seemed fatal. Leaders could exhort followers, followers could persuade supporters, supporters could move onlookers, and you were into two or three thousand people, among whom there would finally be two or three or even one, who would want to make it his own show: a stone, a gun, a bomb. Or you would have a policeman, or several of them, provoking, by innocence or by fault, that very situation many of them had begun to fear as well as relish because it had long since become much more than just an ordinary job.

I had seen the faces of several of the Tac Squad when small units of them marched with that mindless military efficiency of a total blunder to take up a formation before the BSU hut. When they were encircled by a mob of students peeling off from the nearby rally on the open grass of the inner campus, they looked like football players on the sidelines, waiting for the game to begin, for the release into violence. The police made their rushes when the missiles began to fly at them, and I saw black youths scrambling on the peaked roofs of the low surrounding student huts. I thought of Murray's adjuration: guns for self-defense. Anyone on that roof could take one shot, leap off—as some of them were already doing after having hurled a cafeteria tray or a stone—and disappear into the swirling crowd. If I could imagine it, why couldn't the police? Some of them had already drawn guns. Pressed and panicked, how would they have responded to anything that even sounded like a shot?

My anxieties about the unpredictable mounted daily. On one of those embattled afternoons, I was on the corner of Nineteenth and Holloway. I stood among a small group of faculty members. Many of them were union members. We stood between a deep formation of the Tac Squad and a crowd of students who were protesting, with customary obscenities, against arrests that had just been made on the interior campus. Between the students and the faculty, those who had been arrested were being led by other police to the paddy wagons on Nineteenth Avenue. When the watching students came crowding in, we pleaded: "Move back!" "Cool it!" "Don't get close!"

There were television cameras everywhere. A police photographer was taking pictures of us. It was bizarre and it was absurd, and we were almost getting used to it. I was inches away from a Tac Squad officer who held a long club, his black-gloved hands curled tightly around each end of it. His face was expressionless, fathomless, his eyes staring, fixed like two small stones on the mob of students a few feet from him, who raised fists and shouted "Pig!" I glanced at colleagues, I shrugged, I blew my breath, I pleaded with the students to keep back, and I then finally caught the eye of the Tac Squad officer. I needed to say something that might suggest we were but two men in an uncomfortable place, with a shared desire to be somewhere else. But I needed also, I suppose, to show my own cool. I nodded toward the club.

"Is it solid?"

I might as well have asked him about his actual sex. He stared at me. Not a muscle in his face moved. I compelled myself to hold his eyes for as long as he held mine. His face visor was winged up on his helmet; the features of his face were plainly visible. He even had a trim mustache. But I could have been staring at a robot that awaited the next ooze from interior tubing to order its next response. Finally he dropped his eyes to my feet. Then he scanned my height in two quick blinks. He almost smirked. He almost nodded. Again he stared into my face, as if to let me know he was locking it in his mind for that time when he might deliver an illustrating answer to my reckless question. And only then did he turn his head the inch or two to get him back to staring at the students.

"I guess that's my answer," I said to the black man beside me, who taught in the college's Upward Bound program.

"Man," he whispered to me, shaking his head like a grand-father, "there's a time to be just plain quiet. Just have nothing at all to say."

That was it, precisely. There was nothing to say. We were into the essential silence of confrontation. I couldn't reach the man in the cop; he saw nothing but meat in whatever he saw of me. Signifying identities annihilated language. What was there to say of what I had seen and heard in the past few weeks? A plain-clothes man, disguised as a student, but iden-tifiable to any student on the lookout for him, fired two shots to get away from students who had cornered him. Litwak and I watched the wild running toward the explosions and heard the shouts, "A gun! Someone shot! The pigs shot!" I looked skeptically at Litwak, who nodded and said, "Those were gunshots." Another first. I had never been near a gun-shot before. It waited for a campus setting. Sometime during that week I made arrangements to meet my classes at home.

Removing my classes didn't mean I could stay away. I lingered in my office, I wandered out to the campus, I left it when it became something I couldn't watch, I went to meet-ings, and I walked corridors to pick up the latest rumor, the last surmise. Though I taught at home, I spent more hours on the campus than I had during ordinary times. The crisis made its demands, and one form of it, the violence, was casting its own spell.

The more I admitted that a squad of police moving by me on the double with truncheons ready could scare the hell out of me, the more I found it necessary to show up the next day. Anyone could explain what was adolescent in the compul-sion, but other explanations mean more. I had the undenia-ble right to be on the campus where I was employed (indeed, my employers were urging and compelling me to be there), even as I argued that the campus should be closed, and even as I withdrew my class from the campus in order to preserve it as a class. (There was no student unwilling to meet at my home, and those who supported the student strike refused to meet on campus.) But the police who were there to protect my rights inspired more fear than feelings of safety. Since they represented what was lawful, it was intolerable that I should yield to my fear of them.

"Get the hell out of here or we'll kill you!" a cop gone mad had shouted at a student who found herself before two of them on a narrow, isolated pathway where they were enforcing an arrest with drawn guns. The cop who shouted pointed his gun at her. The girl, who had kept herself out of the campus turmoil, had been on her way to class. She fled to her home and cried hysterically. She never came back to the campus. She dropped out for the year.

"My classes are proceeding as normal, and on the campus."

I kept hearing that from various faculty members, and I didn't know what stubborn truth the observation was intended to bolster. Was it moral strength? Political clarity? Educational principle? The student's day on campus didn't begin and end within the confines of any particular classroom. To get from one class to another he often had to walk from building to building on the open campus or on the narrower secluded paths. He might have to do this between the hours of twelve and two, when the disorders were at their peak and full of hazards even for those who designed before they arrived on the campus the day's plan for evasive movement. There were threats of bombs inside the buildings. There was the threat of one's own shredded sense of self. Day by day we felt debased, not only by the brutality itself, but by how we were growing accustomed to it.

"Pig! Pig!" the pretty, well-built girl in a mini-skirt yelled into the face of a 200-pound cop, while his fists tightened around the club and he memorized the features of the long-haired 140-pound youth who stood beside her. When the melee started, the youth was seized. Louder the girl yelled "Pig!" and her friend was clubbed. At the sight of the blood, the girl shrieked. Didn't she expect an opened head to let out blood? A secretary in the School of Humanities whose windows faced Nineteenth Avenue worried that she was going to be shot at by a black sniper firing from windows of the Ecumenical House across the avenue. "Why should they shoot at you?" I asked. "They will! They will!" she cried. A professor of journalism who argued for police and more police to quell the student disrupters stood on the steps of his building and watched the students rallying in front of the Administration Building. He looked at them with merciless contempt. Then someone shouted, "Here comes the Tac Squad!" and he did not walk, but ran like the guiltiest of thieves back into his building.

If there were students and faculty among our silent majority who had seen none of this as they went evasively from one "normal" class to another and then watched it in the evening on TV or read of it in the newspapers, they too were being debased. They could cry their plagues on all the adversaries, or argue that the students who had started it needed now to suffer. But by now, neutrality and even the principle of the necessary enforcement of law and order had no content for me. By now there was no longer a time for rolling issues back to original blame. Debate on that level among ourslves, by December 4, was about as enlightening as a discussion of original sin on a run through a minefield. The explosions had to stop. The scene had to change. The place had to be defused. The police had to be withdrawn. The campus had to be closed. We needed time to become people again, no less an academic community.

I was, of course, in my bleeding heart, as many would say —many of my colleagues among them—yielding to the fascist methods of terror designed by some of the students to paralyze exactly the kind of man my inabilities were proving me to be. I was ready to bear that charge—at least for as long as it might take to reopen the campus on something better than the hallelujah and hell on which we would have closed it. Through which time there were some bloodless things to be done we had not yet tried. Like the student leaders meeting with the trustees, and the governor, and the chancellor.

The powers that prevailed did not share my view. I worked at a state facility financed by and on behalf of the people of the State of California. A state facility, de facto, cannot be closed down, especially not as a response to the turbulent and sometimes violent conduct of some of its students. It certainly cannot be closed indefinitely, or even opened and closed for unpredictable intervals. Continuously through the previous weeks of impasse on the nonnegotiable demands and its consequent heightening of the physical confrontations on the campus, we had heard from the trustees, and from Governor Reagan, and from the chancellor's office about "the people of California." We were being told that they demanded (and this was also nonnegotiable) that come what may on the San Francisco State College campus, it must remain open to fulfill its educational function, and the officers of the state—trustees, governor, chancellor, and the National Guard if need be—were not only committed, but publicly sworn to uphold and execute the will of the more than eighteen million people of the State of California.

It made an image in my mind. I saw, for instance, some four hundred miles to the south, the masses of people in Orange County shouting at me from their swimming pools and from their barbecue pits: "Teach! Teach on that campus up there!" I saw the sparser population, about three hundred miles north in Siskiyou County, weather-hard people, square-jawed, all of them before their television sets, the antennas stuck like hairpins on the mountains, watching on the evening news the turmoil of our distant campus, snapping off their sets in outrage, rising as one to command me: "Damn it all! Stay on that campus down there and teach!" I saw the migrant winos in Stockton strewn on the streets of the section that is there called the "blighted area," uncorking the fifth of Mountain Red, taking one more swig, wiping their cuffs across their mouths, raising their heads, opening an eye, and gurgling at me in unison: "Teach!" The Armenians in Fresno meeting in tribal consort, the farmers in the Imperial Valley, the skiers in Squaw Valley, the citizens of Beverly Hills and the citizens of Dutch Flats were all demanding (nonnegotiably) that I get in there and teach on the campus in my appointed classroom.

The trustees, the governor, the chancellor—they all heard the voices of the people of California. And the people of California were certainly within their rights to speak as they did. They paid the taxes that provided salary for me and tuition-free education for the students of California. And the trustees, and the governor, and the chancellor, in the well-oiled machinery of the entrusted governance of the State of California, were certainly within their rights—and perhaps within the rigid necessities of their duties, not to mention their politics—to express outrage at the unoiled noises of our campus and order me back to teaching in the appointed classroom. After all, they too had television sets on which they could watch the reprehensible disorder. They didn't have to come on campus to see for themselves—and they didn't. And as they ordered me—to complete the image I made—I saw myself not as a teacher, but as a draftee, a conscript. I was the lowest in a military chain of command. Over me was the department chairman, the dean, the vice-presidents, the president, the trustees, the governor, the chancellor, and finally, *all* the people of California, with the exception of myself. And down that long sequential line came the orders, the signed documents, slipping efficiently through the lubricated machine of governance, informing me that, like any other draftee, I would perform my duties even at the risk to myself of injury, even death, and see to it as well that those over whom I had some kind of undefinable command, my students, showed up also for their duties, at the same risks.

Such an image, of course, was nothing more than a product of my "inflamed literary imagination," as someone who had been newly installed in the chain of command above me had already explained a few days before December 4. It was on December 3, though, that my friend George Price bore witness to how inflamed that literary imagination actually was. That was a Tuesday. Shortly thereafter, the day picked up its commemorative tag: Bloody Tuesday.

At about one o'clock in the afternoon of that day I was getting ready to leave my house for the campus when the phone rang. My wife answered it. Listening for a moment, her face drained. She signalled for me to wait. She explained before she gave me the phone that it was Zdena, George's wife. She had just learned he'd been arrested on the campus, taken away in a police wagon. She was frantic. As she was to explain later, her own experience at Auschwitz returned in memories at that moment to confuse her. She forgot about bail. Arrest and a wagon meant transportation. I took the phone and assured her George would soon be home. I would keep calling her. I'd find out where George had been taken, and then we'd go down at once with the bail. I kept calling the Hall of Justice, but the information was always the same. No one by that name had been booked yet.

A friend on the campus called and reported what he'd been seeing. "It's terrible, terrible. The worst day yet. You can't imagine it." I told him about Price. He already knew. He had also heard Price had been beaten by the arresting cops, but he knew none of the details. I spent most of the afternoon on the telephone, until Price was at last booked at the Hall of Justice. The bail was met, and he was released. After dinner my wife and I went to the Prices' house.

He was dazed. He limped badly; his eyes were awful. Tearing, raw, veiny, the lids red and swollen, his eyes and surrounding flesh looked hammered and scraped. His voice was hoarse, his throat red. A white plaster patch the size of a calling card was sealed like a small lid on the crown of his head where the hair had been removed. Through about an hour of talking, and with some of the facts filled in afterward, the story, in bits and pieces, came together.

There had been mayhem on the campus at noontime. Some students had armed themselves with pieces of brick, and one of the thrown objects felled an officer, stretching him on the grass. The police went wild. Charging in squads at knots of students, they whacked away with their clubs. By the time it was over, more arrests had been made, more blood spilled, and more serious injuries inflicted than on any previous day in the past month of confrontations. For a brief while during the melee, Price had been on the open campus between the library and the Administration Building. Walks and a driveway there led to Holloway Avenue, where paddy wagons waited. Two officers of the Tac Squad were hauling a student between them down one of the walks. The student, manhandled, cried out in pain. Price followed at a distance. One of the officers turned his head and commanded Price to get out of there. He did. He stepped off the walk and into the margin of a crowd of onlookers. In a moment, someone behind him pushed him onto the walk again. (A faculty member who had witnessed the event would later testify that it was a student who had deliberately pushed Price forward.)

Price was immediately seized by two other officers of the Tac Squad. One of them got behind Price and used his long club as an immobilizing brace. With a hand on each end, he wedged it against Price's throat while he drove his knee into his back. He pulled with such force on the club that Price, who is six feet tall, was lifted from the ground, his weight suspended from his throat. For a part of the distance to the paddy wagon, he was hauled that way. Before the open doors of the wagon, an officer squirted the unresisting Price with mace. To relieve Price of any delusion he might have had that he'd been mistaken for an over-aged and well-dressed student protestor, a greeting was delivered with the mace: "How do you like that, you fancy pants professor?" No answer was expected, for the greeting was followed by a wallop in the skull with the club. Sagging to the pavement, Price was pulled up and flung into the wagon. He remembered wrenching his knee on the flooring before he passed out for a few moments. The wagon made a stop at the county hospital on the way to the Hall of Justice. One of those delivered to the hospital with Price was a black student named Donald McAllister.

As Price told the story, dabbing his eyes with a handkerchief, he kept interrupting himself with thoughts of McAllister. They fell out in plaintive syllables. "Poor McAllister." "What they did to McAllister." "My God." "Poor McAllister." From its pieces, we put together that story also. Suspected by the police as a brick-thrower, McAllister had been seized by officers of the Tac Squad. Vengefully, mercilessly, they beat him. He was grossly fat, almost neckless, and in the wagon the blood streamed from his head, his ears, his face. His white shirt was soaked with his blood. The next day I was to see a picture of him in the newspaper. A black youth of average height, looking much shorter because of his enormous girth and because his knees are buckled. His short, thick arms are pinned high behind his back by two officers of the Tac Squad. The plastic visor on the helmet of one of the officers is raised. His mouth is parted. He could be smiling, or caught in a grimace of energy. McAllister's eyes are closed, his mouth is stretched wide and deep in a scream of pain. His chin is as low as his chest, and the collar of his white shirt is open, as though no shirt could close around that neck. The shirt is spotted with blood, and the great belly of the shirt is thick with blood. The colossal thighs plunge over the buckled knees. He is a black figure gross in power, shackled, broken, bloody.

He didn't throw a brick, he moaned to Price during the ride in the paddy wagon. He didn't throw anything. He didn't even belong to the BSU. When a squad of cops had charged toward a group of students he was among—some of whom had thrown missiles—he ran. Everyone was running. But he was too fat to run fast enough to get away. And the running, and his size, and where he'd been standing, and his blackness were sufficient evidence on that day. He was judged for it on the spot, and on the spot punished. In the emergency room of the county hospital, Price reported, the pain was too unbearable for McAllister to endure treatment. He cried. The ordeal affected one of the cops in attendance, who was white. Lightly he put his hand on McAllister's naked shoulder.

In the emergency room Price's skull was stitched. The young physician in attendance, on a sewing field day, com-

mented through his ministrations. If all the people of California had taken their stand on what was happening at State,
why shouldn't he? He stitched without any anesthetic, other
than the few observations he offered. "Did the meanie cop
hurt you out there today? Does this hurt you now?" And he
yanked the gut as he drew each stitch. No X-rays were taken.
Price's eyes were perfunctorily treated. He went afterward
for more than a month of treatments to an ophthalmologist.
After a while his headaches disappeared, his throat healed,
and his voice returned to normal. The other effects of that
day lasted a longer time.

A beating is humiliating. One delivered by police in fury
and contempt is all the more so. In this particular context, the
beating rubs your professional life—thought by some to be at
least honorable—in public dirt. Price, moreover, had devoted his life to his profession. He taught his classes passion-
ately, he had personal concern for his students, and he
worked hard at his writing. He had returned to us this fall
after a year of absence. With a publisher's advance, he had
chosen to push for the completion of his novel, but he was
just short of finishing it when the semester began. And that
was to be the end of his writing for a year. He took two
months to recover from the physical effects of being throat-
hauled, maced, and head-busted. It took him longer than that
to put together his life, while he continued his classes at
home, talking about something called fiction, in between
trips to doctors and his lawyer, the latter to defend him
against charges of being on his own campus at the wrong
time and fulfilling the responsibilities of a teacher. The responsibilities were translated by the inflamed fiction of that
day into "interfering with an arrest" and "resisting arrest."

He was eventually to be cleared of those charges, but that
came much later. On campus we organized a fund to help

defray Price's legal expenses. One of the early contributors to it, in cash, was S.I. Hayakawa, the newly appointed acting president, who had already said, among other things, "There are no innocent bystanders."

Hayakawa was appointed by the trustees on the Tuesday preceding the bloody one. The appointment shocked me, it angered me, and when I first learned of it at a School of Humanities emergency meeting, I was not among those who greeted the news with guffaws. I had to wait a long while before I could do that. On November 26, the day of the appointment, I was still trying to reason—if only with myself, and in the glummest of moods. It went like this.

If the Board of Trustees could find their man in Hayakawa so quickly after Smith's resignation, then someone had been selling him to them for some time before that day. The pitch could not have been made through the channels of the college's own Presidential Selection Committee, for it had not been called into session, despite the fact that it was still a standing committee. (Hayakawa was one of the members of that committee, all of whom had agreed that none of them could seek or accept the position of acting or permanent president.) It seemed unlikely on November 26 that many, if any, of the trustees knew anything substantial about Hayakawa. Despite the fact that he was a "world famous semanticist," the Nobel prize had thus far escaped him. Perhaps among the few trustees from the Bay Area, one or two of them might have heard him lecture before a business or professional organization. Perhaps some among the trustees had even read and liked his *Language in Thought and Action*. Perhaps all of them had heard his name and could associate it with that book, or with something called general semantics, or with the college itself.

But surely none of this would have been sufficient recommendation for the acting presidency of the college at this time. Shuffling the papers of Hayakawa's dossier, they must have noted some conspicuous omissions. In his fourteen years at the college he had never had a single administrative job of the smallest kind. For the past dozen years he had not even taught more than part-time. Indeed, they had, to my knowledge, nothing more concrete to go on than the brief, prepared speech Hayakawa had delivered at a full faculty meeting around the time of the convocations. He read it in a quavering voice that took on fiber when it came to the concluding climax in which Hayakawa declared it was his right and duty to teach in his appointed classroom and no violence or threat of violence could keep him from fulfilling that right and duty. Reporters rushed to his side at the end of the meeting, and Hayakawa promised them copies of his speech. Perhaps they were also in his dossier by November 26, or earlier.

That could not have been enough to persuade the trustees within an hour after Smith's resignation, unless the "resignation" had for some time been assumed, and during that time Hayakawa was being promoted, and by that time the job of acting president had been limited to a front man for the immediate and sole purpose of bringing the campus to order through the use of as many policemen as was necessary for as long as was necessary. Reagan had considerable prestige at stake in the execution of this job. As a member of the board of trustees, as the whip among them, he could not be indifferent to the new appointment. Though he himself was scarcely in a position to raise the question of no previous experience, he above all, in one way or another, was the man to sell. I assumed it was Chancellor Dumke who did the selling, and it had to have been primarily Hayakawa who sold himself to Dumke.

The pitch was not hard to reconstruct. A man was being proposed for only the *acting* presidency who was from among S.F. State's own faculty. Moreover, the man was a professor of English from the School of Humanities, a venerable identification in the hard-core sense of the liberal arts. Better than that, this particular English Department and School of Humanities owned the largest hard-core membership of the faculty's troublemakers. Additionally, the proposed man was by name at least as well-known in the academic world as any other member of the faculty. As a special advantage, in addition to everything else, he was a practiced and effective public speaker, with years of experience behind him on the lecture circuit. In that work, which was most often with business and professional organizations, he had met a number of people and made some friends in high places. Were he an official of the college, he might even raise some needed funds. On the racial side, he was a jazz buff and a good friend of Duke Ellington's. Also of Mahalia Jackson's. Better than that, on the racial side, like a windblown gift from the political gods, he was Japanese. The man was actually a birthright member of whatever those students meant by their Third World noise. Surely there was fortunate circumstantial mileage to be gotten out of that. Student rhetoric could invent all kinds of names, but they wouldn't now be able to call the college president a *white* racist. As for the nuisance of the technical side of administrative work, *acting* president, as I heard it on November 26, meant temporary president, and temporary meant some unembarrassing time shortly after the end of the present crisis in its public aspect. Two telephone numbers could suffice for the task: one for the police, one for the chancellor's office. The news media didn't have to be called. They lived on the campus now.

For a short term and specific objective, the trustees bought the product: Hayakawa. That he might be able to deliver the objective was all that mattered. It was a strategy. In turn, the trustees delivered the product to the college, and we had no buyer's choice. But I knew this particular product better than those who had shoved it at me. Hayakawa could not accomplish the short-term objective without bringing long-range ruin to the college itself, not to mention the actual bloodshed I now foresaw as inevitable. So the trustees, and the governor, and the chancellor, acting out of ignorance, or out of dispositions that were fundamentally *radical*, were risking the college in order to gain the battle. But this is the very charge that was directed against the embattled students themselves and that some of their spokesmen publicly admitted to in audacious proclamations in a most unpleasant language. The language of the trustees and the governor and the chancellor was entirely respectable. But their strategy was the same: Never mind the method. Win the battle.

The analogy was inaccurate. Students at their worst would be outside the law. The action of the state power of California could never be, not even at its worst. But it was a time of fire, and the inflamed analogy might be getting at an appropriate distinction. If, in the name of the law and in the manner of respectability, a method was employed that was in itself reckless to the intention of either law or order and the institutions they were meant to preserve, then that lawful method was as destructive as any illegal one. From what I knew of Hayakawa before November 26, I did not expect him to be a college president. I expected him to be a method.

I knew him to be full of vanities. I knew him to be bitter about the academic world and his place in it. He was sentimental; he could even be maudlin. He was paternalistic toward subordinates and solicitous toward those he wanted to impress. He was acutely vulnerable to criticism. Like all of us, he needed respect, esteem, affection; but he had to measure his share in quantities. In his own work he was a salesman who simplified even platitudes. His product was better living through a better understanding of the uses and abuses of language. From the lecture platform, the more corporate the audience, the better the sale. Finally, Hayakawa himself became a part of the product. His pitch was the rational mind. It was capable, once opened and fully functioning, of sparing us private and collective blunder. His goal was success, and he succeeded. Royalties from his *Language in Thought and Action*, originally published in 1941, continued to provide him with a major portion of his income. The observations and insights contained in the book were sufficiently commonplace to be marketplace. His lecture-circuit audiences were usually comprised of those who had visibly succeeded: doctors, dentists, lawyers, psychologists, businessmen, even jazz musicians. His technique as a "generalist" was to talk to doctors about jazz, to musicians about medicine, to lawyers about psychology, to dentists about law. He was a practiced and, in his circuit, effective formal lecturer. His essential style was low-key—the thoughtful, brow-wrinkled pause as the obvious nerve center of the brainwork of rational communication, followed by a platitude dressed in eagerness or humorless wit. His applauding audiences—listeners, or readers of his publications—were of a kind that could be stunned by learning that thought was influenced by language, that values are relative, that categories are falsifying, that the designs of many American cars exploit sex, that Negroes could remain sane even as Negroes if they could exert the strength of mind to ignore that they were Negro.

Banalities like these should hardly have caused any anxieties for the college. Such timidities of intellect could scarcely ruin anything, much less a college. But there was another

factor. Hayakawa was being paid good money for his product. The more he got, the more he sold. The more he sold,
the cheaper it became. The cheaper it was, the more he lost,
among his academic colleagues, of that esteem, respect, and
affection he so much wanted in quantities. It was denied him,
not for envy of the money, but for the quality of the product.
The denial made him think of the academic world—or at
least some parts of it, especially professors of English and
philosophy—as enemy enclaves bristling with alienated intellectual snobs. Against intellectuality in general, he could
be a vindictive man. With power, he could hurt. He had the
right combination of qualities for it: vanity, sentimentality,
bitterness, and energy. I saw some of this on one of the first
occasions that I met Hayakawa.

It was an early fall English Department party not long
after I'd arrived in San Francisco in 1957. I was without a car,
having come to the party with a friend, in the car of a colleague who left early. My friend arranged with Hayakawa for
a lift home. Many drinks later for all of us, Hayakawa was
ready to leave. My friend sat up front with him; I sat in the
back. We wound through the hills of Sausalito, toward the
freeway. Hayakawa did almost all the talking. His voice was
thick; his words came slowly. My friend put in a syllable now
and then, but he was otherwise quiet, looking straight ahead
through the windshield. His silence was an event itself, for in
those circumstances—a few bourbons under his belt and
some minutes to kill in a car—he is a willing and expert
raconteur. On the freeway for the short ride to Mill Valley,
the roles kept up: Hayakawa talking slowly, repetitiously; my
friend mainly silent. We drove at a crawl, and though it was
nighttime and the traffic was light, we moved from lane to
lane. Sometimes we straddled the dividing line. Once we
ground over the gravel of the shoulder. It finally dawned on

me that Hayakawa had done his share of drinking. My friend, I now figured, was silent because it had occurred to him from the beginning. Or because of what Hayakawa was talking about. Or a little of both.

Over and over again, Hayakawa kept on with the same story. It was woe. The great universities had no appreciation of his work. Harvard and Chicago were named particularly and often. A man as well known in his work as he might have expected a chair, at least the ordinary professorship. But the rigidities and snobberies of tradition stood in his way. Because his work crossed through a number of fields, they didn't know in which department to give him a professorship. He *preferred* San Francisco State. A man was allowed his freedom there. The interdisciplinary possibility was encouraged. It didn't matter to him that the college's reputation didn't match those of the Eastern places. It didn't matter. It really didn't. He liked San Francisco State. The Eastern places were full of intellectuals and class snobs.

There were times in his monologue when Hayakawa moved himself to sobs. It might have moved me, too. It could have reached to that embarrassed compassion you save for the humiliated, but I was resentful. He had chosen his world. He had chosen his method in it. It had come to success. He should have relished it. More importantly, I was preoccupied with my own anxieties. I didn't want to get killed on the freeway. Knee-locked and lip-bitten, I endured the ride in an average concern for the continuation of my life, wondering, even as I endured it, why some men did so, why neither my friend nor I could get past the conventional proprieties and take the wheel, not knowing then that some ten years afterward I would again be asking myself why I was allowing my life to be served up to that man's bitter sentimentalities.

Because it was the most telling, that night ride was the

clearest personal recollection I had of Hayakawa. It came to
my mind when I pondered his appointment. Other recollections came too, but not many. I had seldom seen him. I
remembered an evening party at his home for some of us in
the department. We were from the Creative Writing Program, or those closer colleagues of his who taught courses in
semantics, or subjects allied to it, or those who might simply
be friendly to what he was to propose after some drinking.
He asked for our support in the formation of a general semantics institute at the college. The money was to come from
outside sources, mainly business, and the college was merely
to be a place where the institute was housed. Not one of us
who didn't already have something to do with semantics or
who wasn't one of Hayakawa's close friends was very en-
thusiastic. He had finished speaking and there was nothing
but silence or stalling observations from those whose support
he most hoped for. Then a writer colleague took it up. He
ridiculed semantics, the Hayakawa version, and berated
Hayakawa as a popularizer whose huge enrollments in his
lecture courses on campus were comprised mainly of middle-
aged female enthusiasts of the garden club variety. That
ended the business. We milled around with a few more
drinks, and Hayakawa found a harmonica. He went off with
it to a corner and played. And sulked. That night, in a San
Francisco diner, I argued with my colleague and others until
the early hours of the morning. I thought it improper to say
all that to Hayakawa in his own house in front of his wife. My
colleague said "proper" had nothing to do with it.

Hayakawa's appointment on Tuesday fell in the week of the
forthcoming Thanksgiving recess. He advanced the beginning of that holiday by one day; the campus was officially
closed from Wednesday until at least the following Monday.

It allowed Hayakawa the intervening days to plan a method or style of operation before he had to confront the campus in actual session. On Wednesday he met with some of the high administrators of the college, many of them veterans of the confrontations of the year before. To them he proposed some of his ideas for curbing the student uproar and for creating a new atmosphere on the campus when it reopened. The proposals leaked out to some of the faculty. I heard them; I didn't believe them. But the rumors were confirmed for me by an administrator who rolled his eyes and nodded his head as I tallied off what I'd heard. The following were some of Hayakawa's first suggestions as acting president.

Mahalia Jackson was a friend. He'd invite her out to sing from the speaker's platform. He would call for some nuns who would mingle with the students on the open campus, while distributing flowers. He offered the possibility of female law enforcement personnel, from the police department and from the military stationed in the Presidio. He proposed raising money from the Japanese and Negro business communities to create scholarships in the School of Business for Third World students, especially Negroes, who would there learn ways to financial success and thus be better able to cope with the society that estranged them. And he considered the possibility of distributing some emblem—say, blue ribbons—to that vast majority of silent students and faculty who wanted the college to remain open so that the normal educational functions could continue.

Thus the explosion among a generation of college students who were confronting the illnesses of race were to Hayakawa nothing more than a latter-day version of raccoon-coated bootleggers, goldfish swallowers, or pantie raiders. Accordingly, they could be bought off, psyched out, or charmed away. The black student who had heard Cleaver shouting

"Revolution!" at him from the speaker's platform would melt off into sweetness and the Pearly Gates when Mahalia Jackson sang a spiritual to him from that platform. Chicanos and Latinos, some of whom might have been ready to tear down the church itself in the claims they made for their impoverished Spanish-speaking communities in San Francisco, would in the presence of a nun handing them a flower change their chant from "Shut it down!" to "*Ave Maria.*" Of all these initial mind-blowers, the only one Hayakawa could not be dissuaded from was the distribution of the blue ribbons. Which was, of course, a very spirited way to hand out uniforms, and choose up sides, and pick your color.

Early in the Thanksgiving recess, a San Francisco State College student living in Marin County filed for an injunction in a court of that county ordering the college to show cause why it should not reopen and put an end to depriving that student of his education. Hayakawa called a press conference for Saturday at the San Francisco Press Club.

Among those in Hayakawa's audience was Kay Boyle, who had secured a press pass from the editor of a magazine. She rose and asked Hayakawa why he had not chosen a faculty meeting rather than a press conference to inform the college of his plans. He answered that there had already been too many of those faculty meetings. This was a better way. A black reporter rising to ask a question was interrupted by Hayakawa before he could begin. What news medium did he represent? Perhaps, sniffing hostility, Hayakawa suspected false entry. Perhaps he wanted the assembled press to know at once that where liberals were unhappily vulnerable, he was going to be happily tough. Most of the assembled press representatives responded with exclamations of shock and anger. Some wanted to know why Hayakawa allowed every white person to ask his question without such identification.

At the close of the conference, Hayakawa, leaving the room, approached Kay Boyle. She was not unknown to him. Their offices had been close by. Occasionally in the past years he had dropped in to greet her, often remarking how proud he was to be associated with her in the same faculty, the same department. He was smiling as he came toward her now, his arms extended in greeting. Locking her arms behind her back, Kay Boyle refused to accept the greeting. She told him he had betrayed the faculty.

Early on Monday morning, Hayakawa arrived at the reopened campus. Two student protestors had already parked a small truck on Nineteenth and Holloway. When students started arriving for eight o'clock classes, they were greeted with messages blaring over the loudspeakers mounted on the truck. Some faculty members, including Kay Boyle, had also arrived early to distribute leaflets in support of the student strike and condemning the autocratic appointment of Hayakawa. There were also some students loaded with the blue ribbons that they were trying to give away without much success. The silent majority wasn't about to surrender the security of its silence.

On his way to his new office in the Administration Building, or already in it, Hayakawa heard the loudspeaker. It was in direct defiance of his edict against this use of amplification equipment, assuming that the curbside at Nineteenth and Holloway was a part of the campus. One thing Hayakawa certainly assumed: direct physical confrontation, regardless of the possible consequences, was better than prolonged ambiguities. It was a view that had always been advanced by the striking students. Perhaps he also assumed there just might be some cameramen on that corner. The rumor was already out, which was soon to be confirmed by a report in the San Francisco *Chronicle*, that Hayakawa's millionaire friend, W.

Clement Stone, had provided him with ten thousand dollars to hire a Bay Area public relations expert for his own use, supplementing the PR staff already on the college's payroll. Hayakawa, accompanied by the plain-clothes bodyguards assigned to him by the police department, bedecked in a piece of what he might have meant by sartorial diversity, a tam-o'-shanter, hustled off toward the busy corner and the sound truck.

He demanded that the students cease this violation of his order. The students were certainly surprised to see him, but they refused to comply. The surprise turned to amazement when Hayakawa, a short man, in his early sixties, scrambled atop the hood of the truck, and then onto the roof. A student in the truck, recovering from his shock, went up after Hayakawa. For a moment they jostled each other. The student protested the abuse of his property. Hayakawa stood his ground, which was his little square of the metal rooftop. The quickly gathered assemblage stared up at him. Now what? He was beginning to speak. Adorned in the tam-o'-shanter, short, bespectacled under triangulated eyebrows, with mustache over a mouth that twitched into grins, the newly-appointed acting president, or interim president, with the cameras indeed clicking and grinding, there on the corner that was the very emblem of our streetcar college, as if he himself were a revolutionist practiced for years in street-side, truck-top oratory, Hayakawa was about to speak. But he no sooner started, when the student with the microphone began his harangue again. It bellowed on the loudspeakers. Hayakawa's mouth moved, but there was nothing to be heard from it. There was only the barking from the large metal funnels.

Infuriated, still on the roof of the truck, Hayakawa found the wires leading to one of the loudspeakers. He reached down, hauled them up, and tore them loose. Again the shouts of "Private property!" supported now by protests and registrations of shock from those gathered on the corner before the truck. Among them was the voice of Kay Boyle, who had once, on assignment for the *New Yorker*, covered the trials in Frankfurt of Nazi war criminals.

"Hayakawa - Eichmann!   Hayakawa - Eichmann!"   she shouted.

"Kay Boyle, you're fired!" Hayakawa, trembling, flung back at her.

He was eased down from the truck by the protesting students. In the crowd, he was jostled again. "Keep your hands off me," he screamed. "I'm the college president!" He began throwing blue ribbons into the crowd of gawking onlookers. Escorted by his bodyguards, he finally made his way back to his office in the Administration Building to take up some of the other responsibilities of his new job. He was later to deny that he had shouted anything at Kay Boyle that would suggest he was firing her, and offered at subsequent times differing versions of what he believed he had actually said. When the crowds on the corner eventually dispersed, Tac Squad officers arrested the students identified with the truck.

By the end of the day marked by rallies, confrontations, and violence, Hayakawa had suspended five of the student strike leaders. One was the head of the SDS; the others belonged to the BSU and TWLF. Most of them had taken part in the convocations. In Sacramento, Governor Reagan, assessing the day and referring to Hayakawa, said, "I think we have found our man."

And then there was Bloody Tuesday. And George Price was poleaxed. And McAllister was shredded. And in the late afternoon of that Bloody Tuesday, Hayakawa, in a press conference in his office, sporting a lei that he reported was a gift from his admirers off campus, talked about roller coasters.

On Wednesday afternoon the A.F.T. held a meeting in a church near the campus. I attended. Someone at the door was handing out membership cards. I took one and filled it out and turned it in before the meeting began. I joined the A.F.T. without any liberating sense that I was signing up for actual collective power. The union membership was too few in number for that. I joined, knowing that as a Johnny-come-lately I would, by temperament, say and contribute little. That was all right, too. I might be silent, but I was not going to be alone. I couldn't if I wanted to. I was now grateful the union was there. If I wasn't in it, I'd be accepting the Hayakawa appointment, and his violent inspirations.

The word *collaborator* now became a part of my own rhetoric. The A.F.T. was not only an active form of opposition, it was, as well, a way out of collaborating. It was a relief from the dismay I was still capable of when, a week after the Hayakawa appointment—it being clear to all of us by then how Hayakawa would administer the college, and to what authority in Los Angeles and Sacramento he was immediately committed, and to what gross self-promotion he was ultimately compelled—when, in the face of that, there was no flood of resignations from department chairmen, and deans, and high administrators. There was nothing. Among the greatest number there was only general gloom.

My major complaint wasn't that Hayakawa had taken a hard line. After Smith's resignation, we could hardly expect a soft or moderate one, whomever the trustees appointed to replace him. My outrage was against the character and style of the man who stood for that line. Neither in his person nor through his actions could there be the beginning of a way toward solution. He was a method. He was selling again. To do it all the more effectively for the limited ends he served, he provoked. Whatever else the campus chaos had been to any of us, it was publicly admitted by Hayakawa to be roller coaster fun for him.

If the trustees knew this essential side of the man even as they appointed him, they were themselves provocateurs. If they knew nothing of this side of the man, they were wondrously negligent. But Governor Reagan had already approved: "I think we have found our man." The power of the state, in the name of the public, had turned to public agitation.

When I joined the union, I took with me my outrage against this provocative power: the trustees, the governor, the chancellor, and their "right" man, Hayakawa. It remained to be seen, regardless of immediate public opinion, on which side was the greater threat to the public—with those empowered, or those who protested the uses of that power, faculty members now as well as students. But in joining the union, I didn't for a minute believe that I was supporting all of the demands of the striking students or even endorsing the methods they had chosen to pursue those demands. But neither did you have to subscribe to the Yippies in Chicago to be sickened by what had been done against so many of them, and all of us.

9 · Christmas time
Part I - LEO LITWAK

My father was a union man and out of deference to him I had joined the college chapter of the American Federation of Labor. My membership remained entirely casual, however. I didn't vote in elections. Dues were subtracted from my paycheck, and I received insurance discounts and other benefits. That was the extent of my involvement.

A handful of dedicated labor people among our ranks kept the union going. They achieved only minor success in campaigning for collective bargaining, a lighter teaching load, and a new grievance procedure. While many professors were sympathetic with these objectives, few subscribed to labor tactics.

But with the crisis that followed the end of the convocation and the appointment of Hayakawa, the time of the union had arrived. The purely academic institutions had failed us. None of them had an apparatus for mounting an effective protest. The Academic Senate was powerless. The faculty assembly passed resolutions that were ignored. The convocation had clearly established that we were too divided for action as a college. The ad hoc committee lacked any organization for a sustained protest. Only the union, with its labor connections, and its labor strategies, provided an answer to our obvious disorder.

The union announced it would strike if the Hayakawa appointment were not withdrawn. Reagan and Hayakawa put an invidious face on the union involvement, calling it opportunistic, denouncing the union leaders as provocateurs and malcontents. They were especially outraged by the timing of the union threat, coming as it did while the college struggled with the student strike. The fact is that if the strike provided the A.F.T. with an opportunity to increase its power, it was because faculty grievances were intensified and a sizable number of professors were ready for extreme measures to find relief.

I wasn't sanguine about the outcome of a faculty strike. I hoped the threat of one would be sufficient to force the trustees to yield power to the college. Even as I supported the measures that would result in a faculty strike, I didn't really believe it would come to that. I hoped that our preliminary preparations would break the stalemate and force both students and trustees to negotiate. Most of those in the union aimed for a limited objective—hoping to restore the campus to normal operation on the basis of faculty resolutions. There would be an Ethnic Studies School, a Black Studies Department, and a much larger enrollment of minorities. We also wanted to affirm our right to answer student demands in any future crisis. That was actually to want a great deal, but we were ready to settle for less.

The militant unionists pushed us strikeward, arguing—correctly, I think—that we would gain nothing by mere bluff, that we deluded ourselves if we imagined there was any alternative to a test of strength. There was a faction that believed our primary goal was to support the student strike until the fifteen demands were satisfied. Another faction, comprising most of the union leadership, took the labor movement seriously and believed a strike could establish our fraternity with labor, and only then would professors gain the power to control the college. Both factions were agreed that mere threat would not be sufficient and they led the majority of us, who were timid, in the direction of a strike.

The first step was to secure the approval of the San Francisco Labor Council. This meant submitting a list of griev-

ances whose legitimacy the council would have to determine. Our attorney, Victor Van Bourg, advised us to express
our grievances in language that labor men could understand.
The implication was that we should not flaunt our connections with the student strike. Labor chieftains shared the
public sentiment in regard to the student strike. To get strike
sanction from them we had to formulate strike demands that
were independent of the students'. Van Bourg, who was also
a Labor Council attorney, indicated that labor leaders were
justifiably suspicious of our prior aloofness from the labor
cause. We would have to persuade them that we were in this
for legitimate labor objectives. It was unnecessary to utter
everything we stood for. That might be morally admirable
but tactically foolish. Van Bourg didn't pretend to know what
our relations to the Third World were. But he urged us to
devise our tactics with regard to the facts of power. We
couldn't rely on legal maneuvers, since the courts were as
subject as any other institution to political influence, and our
cause was not popular. Nor could we rely on any agreement
with the trustees. Such agreements would last only if we had
the muscle to support them. Our power rested on the
strength of the union and its labor movement allies.

Van Bourg was a comfort to those who opposed unequivocal support of the student strike as self-defeating. We didn't
want assurance of total victory in order to act, but we surely
didn't seek the disaster of a total defeat. The majority of the
union members favored the hard-headed, unideological
course recommended by Van Bourg and stressed the value
of a labor alliance.

We conducted our meetings at a time when campus battles
were bloodiest. The student leaders wanted us to come to
their aid immediately without waiting for strike sanction.
BSU and Third World representatives—some of them union

members because they held teaching assignments—audited our meetings. They were suspicious of our pursuit of labor affiliation. They condemned the Labor Council as a bourgeois Establishment power. They saw our request for strike sanction as a desire for respectability that was in opposition to their own revolutionary goals.

We agreed to a trial run that would compromise no one, neither those eager for immediate battle nor those who wavered. We secured clearance from the administration to mount an informational picket line in front of Hayakawa's office. It would not be a strike action. It would not require Labor Council sanction. It would, at the same time, demonstrate to the students our commitment to the principle of the fifteen demands.

Close to two hundred of us assembled near Hayakawa's office. We circled between two files of highway patrol. The police made themselves stony. They refused to banter with us. Their eyes bored straight ahead. At the same time, the students assembled in the commons a hundred yards away, thousands of them, easily worked up by speakers after several weeks of bloody conflict. The police didn't trust them near Hayakawa's office. The moment the students would start moving, the ring of police surrounding the commons— more than six hundred strong—would close in for more bloody work. I was relieved to be in an orderly line that was no problem to police. The students meant to be provocative. They itched to see justice done after the bloodletting they'd witnessed. They intended to use up all the free play the police allowed them and then push across the boundary into forbidden ground. We reassured the police by our decorum that we were professorial and harmless. There wasn't a "pig" uttered by our line. In fact, there was the sort of academic talk which would remind anyone who overheard that we were professors and governed by proprieties.

We were engaging in actions that were brand-new to us and many of us had to act against our fear. We exposed ourselves to the kind of risk we had never imagined we could take. Eventually we were able to circle between the tensed ranks of police without the skin-prickling expectation that a cop might start flailing away. Our picketing would have gone on so for an hour and we would then have returned to more characteristic academic behavior, but the word came via author Kay Boyle that the students feared a Tac Squad assault and wanted our protection.

I had already decided that it was foolish to assume that we had that kind of power. We weren't priests. It's a myth, for instance, that the red cross insures neutral status. Several medics in my battalion during the war were killed even though they flaunted the red cross. Eventually, I muddied up my own shoulder brassards so that the crosses would no longer be targets.

Did Kay Boyle believe in magic? Did she believe that everyone would fall back in awe of our column, while we defined a circle between students and cops that no one would dare violate? No. She simply refused to hold herself in check when she decided what was just action. She was resolved not to be a good German and to remind everyone that they were not immune to becoming good Germans.

So, despite the agreement that our line wouldn't be involved in the student demonstration, we followed Kay Boyle toward the hot action in the commons. The students cheered and opened a corridor for us through the densely packed crowd that surrounded the speaker's platform. We trudged through grounds drenched by sprinklers, in order perhaps to discourage the use of the commons. We marched straight as arrows into that hip assembly of beards and bandannas and jeans and berets and sombreros, attended by the enthusiasm that greets the home team as it enters the field through a corridor of cheerleaders. A young lady afterward gripped my hand and said, "Thank you! Thank you! I know what you risked!" It was stunning to be inside that crowd's passion. They were so tuned to each other that in an instant they could mount a chant in a single roar, not so much obedient to the amplified voice of their leader as following his articulation of their own common impulse. Above the roar I could hear the familiar echo of the public address system on top of the Administration Building, broadcasting the inappropriately pedantic voice of Hayakawa, which identified the opposing sides and warned us against the wrong choice. These broadcasts of Hayakawa were amazing. They weren't the simple, neutral, mechanical instructions of a police officer, but mini-lectures, a surprising cool in the midst of all that heat. Whatever I denied the man, I couldn't deny him a knack for irony. He had a brazenness which—if I were on his side of the quarrel—I could view as courage.

When the speaker shouted, "Hayakawa forbids obscenity," the thousand students turned in the direction of Hayakawa's office and pumped their fists up and down, chanting spontaneously, "Fuck you! Fuck you!"

I hid behind my sign. To paraphrase the punch line of an old joke, "To a college president you say, 'Fuck you'?"

A middle-aged lady standing beside me, a professor specializing in the education of English teachers, clutched her picket sign as if she were about to go under, blanching at the obscenity.

The students continually forced us toward a deeper commitment than we wanted to make. They demanded that we accept their whole slate and it seemed too much for us. Our informational picket line terminated in the heart of the

crowd. How could we settle for "fuck you" when it would
jeopardize the discipline that went, for instance, into devel-
oping the education of English instructors? This public obscenity seemed to require of many of us that we renounce all
our connections with our professional careers. The students
wanted us to burn our bridges and move toward the side of
revolution. But we were having a hard enough time deciding
on a strike. Every step we took seemed to carry us further
from our professional existence.

On December 13, Hayakawa got all the waverers off the
hook. He suddenly announced the premature beginning of
the Christmas vacation, three days before the union was to
vote on an immediate strike action, without waiting for Labor Council sanction. He announced as his reason the need
for a cooling-off period, during which time our disrupted
community might be conciliated. He also feared a rumored
invasion of the campus by militant high school students.

We had no doubt that our imminent strike vote was the
main reason for closing the college. Most of us welcomed the
decision, which, nonetheless, seemed blatantly hypocritical.
Hayakawa had done precisely what many of us had been
vainly urging. Smith had been forced to resign because of his
refusal to keep the college open under any condition.
Hayakawa had come into office insisting that he would never
be intimidated into closing the college. He was ready to let
the police go all the way. He refused to indulge "anarchists"
and "hoodlums." He had mocked our desire to suspend operations in order to talk. Now he did what we had asked, but
used semantic cunning to disguise the fact. Instead of "closing the college" he had merely "extended the vacation."

There would now be three weeks for the Labor Council to
attempt mediation between the A.F.T. and the trustees. It
was obvious that the mediation would have to involve the

student demands. But Governor Reagan remained adamantly opposed to negotiation. Our union leaders expected that the Labor Council's efforts at mediation would fail and that when school resumed on January 6 we would receive strike sanction and our strike would begin.

Part 2 - HERBERT WILNER

During the Christmas recess to which Hayakawa had so egregiously added a week, I found possibilities for convalescence. I began again to work on my novel, which was under contract and overdue. I met at my house with several students who were completing creative writing projects for their M.A. theses. My children, on their own vacations, filled the house with friends. I watched football on television. I read. But much of this work and distraction was like the doomed effort to overcome a serious illness by ignoring it.

The mail brought reports from the union about the failures of the mediation procedures. Colleagues on the telephone relayed facts, rumors, speculations about Third World student leaders who weren't being nudged into negotiation or concession because they were finding no one to meet with who was empowered to deliver them anything. Statements by Reagan and Hayakawa continued to provoke. Occasional union meetings assumed the inevitability of a strike. In some philosophically abstract structure, I still had choice for the role I would decide to play—I could still duck out. But the process in which I was caught wasn't abstract. The only corner left for me was in the hope that the illness would go away during the recess, or at least remit. But the days went by, the failures accumulated, my corner got tighter, my work on the novel feeble.

The irony didn't escape me. What I had twenty years ago so rationally and cautiously chosen—the secure life that would provide its own mild rewards as well as the time for writing—was no longer secure or even rational. The fights I had chosen for years not to fight were choosing me. And now I was actually in a labor union I had always snubbed, and it was preparing a strike that raised questions to which there were no answers. How long were we going to be out on the line, and the limb, when the students, with three calm weeks for coming to terms, had come to nothing? Could we succeed in closing the campus? In curtailing the violence? What prices were we going to pay? How prepared was I to pay mine? What was to become of the college?

At the end of the holidays, the one question on which all others depended was to be answered at the union meeting held on Sunday evening, January 5, twelve hours before classes were to resume. We were, finally, out of time, out of possibilities for student settlements, for frantic and unreal talk with conciliatory but unempowered citizens committees, with unempowered trustee representatives who happened to live in the Bay Area, with appointed but unempowered federal negotiators, with ad hoc or "concerned" faculty groups trying to fling a rope across a gulf. We were out of everything but the one announced purpose of the meeting: a strike vote.

We voted for the strike. We voted for it to begin immediately. The vote was unanimous. The fervor with which the strike endorsement was received—the applause, the stamping of feet, the shouts of "Right on!"—were not expressions of enthusiasm, but relief. The tensions of building up to the strike, of trying to answer the questions in advance, were at last over. We were momentarily exuberant with our dramatic release into the future uncertainties of the act itself.

About six of the BSU leaders were at the meeting. They were apart from us, standing against the wall at the rear of the room. Some of them wore sunglasses and field jackets. They observed the climactic strike vote without expression. During the proceedings they had whispered to each other; occasionally one or two of them smiled at something privately revealed. Otherwise they were almost sullen.

Immediately after the strike vote, an A.F.T. member brought to the floor the matter of off-campus teaching during the strike. I was unprepared to discuss it. I hadn't expected it to become a formal issue so soon. I had assumed it was to be individually decided, at least at the beginning. I was to learn later that the union's executive board thought it a loaded and prematurely divisive problem, and that a decision about it was best postponed for a while. They had hoped before the meeting that the issue of teaching wouldn't come up. The arguments on both sides grew harder, the words hotter, the list of speakers longer. Before we could raise our first sanctioned picket sign, we had to decide what kind of strike we were to be picketing for. The very options we had for such a decision marked how different we were from the organized labor we were depending on to help us through.

Those who opposed off-campus teaching argued that we couldn't expect real support if we chose for the Mickey Mouse operation that assured our pay while we called ourselves strikers. Our commitments had to be unqualified, and we had to expect our students to pay their price, too. Besides, there were practical considerations: not everyone could make practicable arrangements for teaching off-campus.

The countering arguments limited the strategy of the strike to the closing of the campus. Off-campus teaching did not contradict that strategy. Most practically, a strike had to recognize financial survival. There was no strike kitty. Those who could continue their salaries by off-campus teaching should do so. They could contribute financially to those who couldn't. As for the students, they should not involuntarily pay the price of our strike. For many of them, the immediate future depended upon the completion of the semester.

The debate went on and on toward a vote that, obviously, would not be unanimous this time. Then the chairman called from the list of speakers the name of one of the BSU leaders. We all turned in our seats. When the speaker finished, he yielded not to the list, but to another of the BSU members, and he the same. No one in the faculty shouted for getting back to the list, and the black students went on, ringing all the notes. It was a prepared fusillade for an issue they apparently would have forced had it not already been raised. According to them, there was to be no teaching anywhere, period. They were asserting again their leadership of the campus rebellion. No matter how broadly the rebellion spread—and they urgently wanted it spread—it was first of all *their* scene. And as they spoke, they marked it off, one subject after another, one speaker following another.

The ghettos. Did any of us in our middle-class white man's living know what it was like in there? Know it in the way of having lived it? The poverty, the filth, the rats, the dope, the no way out. Did we know what a revolution was about? Did we know the meaning of putting our bodies on the line? It didn't mean backing up a white liberal gesture with a paycheck at the end of the month. It didn't mean worrying about the white kids finishing their semester at the college when Blacks in the ghettos had no chance of getting into that college in the first place, Blacks who'd be the only hope, educated and trained, for doing something about the ghetto. How did we come around, anyway, to taking a vote on the strike and everyone right on for it and the next minute talk about teaching all the same irrelevant bullshit off-campus so that white kids put nothing on the line, lost nothing, and got their little grades while we got our checks? To put our bodies on the line was to know where Third World students were at, and we weren't going to know it any other way.

Finally, one of the BSU leaders finished it. He leaned forward, he angled his body, he stretched his arm, the index finger pointing. He swept the room, settling finally on the officers of the union up front. He spoke as loudly and plainly as the theater director would have wanted. If you teach anywhere, he said, we'll stop it. We'll come after you. It don't matter who you are. And we'll hold this executive board responsible. We'll come with guns and get you. We'll get machine guns and get all of you. There ain't going to be any teaching!

It went something like that. It took the breath away. The question was called for. The vote was about four to one against any teaching.

The ill-timed audacity of this version of the black rhetoric stunned me. It wasn't my dismay at how the vote went. I doubt that the subsequent vote was anything but adversely influenced by the threats. Indeed, a handful of A.F.T. members went out of the strike and out of the union right then and there. I myself was going to continue off-campus teaching, and so were most of the others who voted to do so. And the students disdain for my salary, wasn't the entire source of the shock. Most of us understood that the administration would maneuver to cancel the pay of faculty who didn't formally disassociate themselves from the strike, but would, when that time came, still continue to teach. What hurt was the assumption by the Blacks of how many lessons I still had to learn, and that last empty and ugly threat one of them had chosen for his idea of effective instruction. I hadn't expected they would congratulate us, or welcome us. Neither did I expect the bullshit.

I had jumped step by step and push by push toward the union and the strike not because of *them* specifically, the black students at S.F. State, one by one, and their demands, each by each. Their outburst at the meeting, in retrospect anyway, only suggests how high on their public hook they were, how drenched they must have been with alternating moods of utter disaster and its obverse, the delusionary conviction of a complete triumph in Reagan's California. I was into the strike—and inevitably so, and BSU behavior couldn't get me out of it—not so much by what I was clearly for but by what I was so angrily against. To proceed as usual was to collaborate, and that was, by this time, an impossibility.

This conviction was shared by everyone in the A.F.T., whatever the many and crucial differences we individually held. We took it into the strike with us, and for many of us the conviction kept us out there beyond our own expectations and abilities. We also took that strike-vote meeting with us. It had made plain how alone we were. We were "with" the black students, but not among them. They wouldn't have us. If they hadn't started what they did, we would not be on strike. If they could come to the end of their strike, we'd surely lose the impetus for our own. But for as long as they remained on strike, it would be difficult, even humiliating, to settle our own. Our causes were now, to a great extent, independent of theirs; but our latitudes as strikers were tied to their intentions as strikers. And they refused, with their necessary arrogance, the human associations that were ordinarily inherent in such a tie. We were exquisitely alone.

The overpowering isolation in the midst of what we simultaneously began more and more intensely to share as a small band of faculty strikers was to become the essential experience for me of the strike and the picket line. It was going to be—as the black students had shoved it at me during the meeting—another lesson to learn.

10 · a Kafka strike

HERBERT WILNER

When I was a boy I felt sorry for the men I saw carrying signs that said "On Strike." They walked back and forth in front of markets, small shops, and stores. They always looked shabby and unwanted, and even, except for moments of anger, a little ashamed. Sometimes, in those small neighborhood strikes to which my experience was limited, I saw a man come out from inside the place and curse the pickets. The strikers yelled back. Then the man went inside again, and the men with the signs had to keep walking back and forth, going nowhere. I knew they picketed to keep people from buying in the store, and I knew, or guessed, they wanted to be paid more. I even imagined they were ashamed to make it known publicly that they weren't already earning enough. But what really moved me to pity was that they were grown men and they had nowhere to go. They walked back and forth in front of the store or the shop as a way of asking others not to go in, but they were outside and couldn't go in either. Not even when it was bitter cold, not when it snowed or rained. When the strike finally ended, the men were back inside again. And then I couldn't understand how they could so easily talk with, and work with—as if nothing had happened—the man who had once come out to curse them.

Thirty years later I was on the picket line, myself shut out from my place of work. I taught my classes at home, and in one of them Kafka was the subject. We talked about the qualities that made Kafka funny, and it wasn't hard to imagine what he could have done with the material of the strike. Every day the events at the college challenged the logic of a sensible world. While I walked the picket line, for instance, and became absurd to myself, all the Kafka machinery of officialdom continued its own funny course. The unwhite but not black Hayakawa met in Washington with President Nixon to exchange views on higher education in America. Governor Reagan in Sacramento—formerly George Gipp of Notre Dame, and various cowboys—spoke of bayonets for campus peace. And Chancellor Glenn S. Dumke in Los Angeles, author of the potboiler that didn't make the best-seller list, *The Tyrant of Baghdad*, denounced the unprofessional conduct of the faculty strikers.

When I was young and read Kafka for the first time, I was terrified. I saw nothing funny in him. My own students—older than I was, in a world much older than mine was—are never surprised when they learn that Kafka was seized with laughing fits when he read from his manuscripts. My students laugh too. And they would have laughed for the same reasons had I recounted to them some of the events I witnessed during the faculty strike. Sometimes, recounting them to my wife or to a colleague, I laughed. Sometimes I was only grim.

There was, for instance, the young professor, bearded, hot-blooded, good at linguistics, an admirer of Johann Kepler. His picket station was at the entrance to the student parking facility. Scarfed and red-nosed in the raw cold, he flagged down cars and tried to talk the students out of entering. One particular car, a red Mustang, was filled with Chinese youths who had probably escaped Chinatown on the backs of fathers working twelve hours a day. The professor talked and talked, raising his voice against the stony silence inside the car. As the car began to move onto the campus, he ran alongside it, panting, shouting union explanations. Then the car roared away. The exasperated prof, his mouth gumming on the phrases that were still unsaid, finally erupted with the terrible indictment: "You racist bastards!"

There was the student, a striker—male, white, young, long-haired—doing theater on the corner of Nineteenth and Holloway, with one of the mounted cops staring down at him from the height of his wheeling, ass-muscled horse. The cop, in a black leather jacket, was red-faced and burly. He sat on the horse the way he must have stood at a bar, ramrod, mean-eyed. He stared and stared at the student until the student finally asked him, but with the slightest smirk, "What are you looking at?" He got no answer, only the ruthless look, and so repeated the question again while the student pickets marched back and forth chanting, "On strike! Shut it down!" and the cop finally said, "I heard what you said before." The student, wide-eyed, the slight smirk still visible, laid his hand innocently to his chest and said, "Me? I didn't say anything. What did I say?" And the cop said, "I heard you," and the student disclaimed, "I never said anything," and the cop, forced, glancing around him, was finally made to say it himself: "You said, 'Look at the ass on the horse.' " The student grinned from ear to ear, until the cop suddenly leaned down and hissed between locked teeth: "Wait till it starts. I'll get you, you little sonofabitch. I'll get you." And the student backed off a step, the smile fading. He backed another step, and then turned altogether and weaved down Nineteenth Avenue, through the line of pickets, until he disappeared.

The occasional sense of danger, the public color, and the Kafka-funny incidents of the picket lines were almost always on Nineteenth Avenue near the corner of Holloway. There, on rare sunny afternoons, a few young women of the BSU danced to rock music, flaunting their bodies before a rigid platoon of the Tac Squad. The girls teased maliciously when they found a cop who didn't smile, whose mouth stretched into a scar while he watched the dancers, his hands grinding around his truncheon.

On Nineteenth Avenue a Japanese professor of anthropology, in the gaudy costume of a Samurai warrior, paraded
with a sign that read something like this: "All Japs may look
alike, but they don't think alike."

And a tall black man not of our campus, supposedly a med
student, in his late twenties and resembling Stokely Carmichael, walked the line with two nervous Doberman pinschers
on tight leashes. We heard the dogs were trained to challenge uniformed cops, and one of the cops had obviously
heard it, too. When he was snarled at, he maced both dogs.
They collapsed immediately, yowling in terror and pain.

And there was always the mystery of what prompted the
police in one instance to go after a student for whom they
had an outstanding warrant, but not to go after him in another instance. Often the student they were after was in a
thick line of picketing students who didn't even know what
the police charge was all about. So the push, the shove, the
clubs, the little bit of mayhem, and the faculty pickets pleading for calm.

On that corner I saw a group of phys. ed. students smash
faculty picket signs placed against a tree. They were observed by a young instructor. Raised in Brooklyn, educated
at Amherst and Yale, he once confessed to me that he was
essentially a private and bookish person who had no taste for
department committees and college politics. Now he was on
strike. He was tall and well-built, and the Brooklyn imprint
showed through when he protested the sign-smashing.
"What are you doing? What the hell do you think you're
doing?" he shouted to the students. One of them rushed
through a squad of cops, shoved the instructor, then retreated into the cops' wedge. The cops, who had ignored the
sign-smashing, closed ranks to prevent the instructor from
getting at the student. One of the cops, full of unexplainable

fury, using his club as a brace, pushed the instructor back. "Get him out of here or I'll bust his head open!" the cop yelled. Witnessing faculty intervened. The picketing resumed, but the young instructor, trembling, walked back and forth with tears in his eyes.

There was the daily conversation I kept hearing between two cops assigned to the same picket station. They were both tall, both in their late twenties. One of them was wiry, probably well-muscled and athletic. He could stand for a long time in one place without moving much. He smiled easily. The other was heavier. In his adolescence he was probably overgrown and clumsy. He was pale, restless. Often he struck a gloved hand with his club, or rapped his heel, or the curbstone. He glanced at men as if he needed to know at once whether he could take them. The wiry man seemed the more tolerant. I overheard him uphold dissent but oppose violence. The pale, heavier cop insisted that one led to the other and where do you draw the line? Their exchanges got shorter, sharper. The pale cop asked his buddy, "Did you get into a lot of fights when you were a kid?" "Some," the wiry cop said. "Did you win all of 'em?" The wiry cop shrugged. The pale cop tilted his head, squinted, and then asked in a flat voice humming with repressed feeling: "Did you go all out? Did you want to win bad enough to fight dirty? Would you knee the sonofabitch in the balls?"

As a picketer I was subject very often, especially in the cold or the rain, to a prosaic woe: I had to pee. The cure should have been simple, but I needed certified permission from a picket captain in order to enter the nearest building of the forbidden campus. On a particular day, I encountered a captain carried away by his duties. Squirming, I was actually expected to defend my private need as an A.F.T. emergency. It was the only legitimate reason for issuing a pass. I was advised about neighboring bushes, a quick one-mile run to union headquarters, until, bursting, I cried, "Fuck you and your bushes!" I entered the campus and the building without the damned pass. And in the john I felt only mixed relief. I kept staring at the trash can, waiting for the hidden bomb to blow the hell out of the can and the john and me.

The union meetings were held in a Y. in the Fillmore, where street-wise black kids jammed the coin return of the empty coke machines and one of my strike colleagues, who'd gone gung ho for labor, urged us at almost every meeting to show up on weekends at the picket line of striking oil-refinery workers at Richmond, across the bay. At one meeting, in a passion of alliance and fraternity, he recommended we turn in our oil company credit cards, on the spot. That was the way, I thought, to scare the life out of barons whose empire stretched to Arabia. What next? I couldn't get a salary. I didn't, technically, have a job. I couldn't enter my own campus. I couldn't pee. I couldn't buy grapes. I couldn't shop at Safeway because they sold grapes. I couldn't go to certain movie houses because the janitors were on strike. Now they wanted my gasoline card.

If there were times when the union failed to recognize that most of us were only college teachers and not laborers or passionate unionists, there were also times when the union carried on like a boys' club instead of acting with the toughness of labor. We were well into the strike and had already missed a salary check when we learned that a member of our executive board had received his paycheck for January. He could not have gotten it without signing the administration's newly instituted vouchers, requiring us to certify that we had fulfilled our academic responsibilities. This act betrayed union policy. He submitted a *mea culpa* statement to the union. He referred to the size of his family, his debts, the sheer impossibility of living without income. He offered his resignation from the executive board, but he was resolved to remain on strike. He would not again put in for salary.

He attended the meeting at which we were supposed to act on the matter, and in his presence there was no easy way of getting at the nasty business. Finally, from the floor came a surprising motion to reject the resignation. It was unanimously approved. What was worst in our comrade was preferable to the best in our enemy, and in the name of unity we confessed weakness. We were capable of making our own Kafka material.

The strike lasted for eight weeks, during a raw and rainy season. We reacted to it with a remarkably collective will, lasting longer in our determinations than even we had any right to expect of ourselves. For me, after several weeks of the strike, the drain was severe. Unable to swallow the absurdities, unable to expel them by laughter, my anger grew and grew, but the picketing, which, in its very boredom, fed the anger, was not an activity through which I could work it off.

I was on the line, in the most literal and functioning sense, to inhibit others from entering the campus. At the same time that I tried to inhibit, I was myself prohibited. The longer I was locked out of the campus while others were free to come and go despite my dutifully emblematic efforts, the more irrationally I began to think of the campus as rightfully mine. I had never before, I believed, excessively identified myself with the college; but now, on strike against it, it became— and very personally—*my* territory.

Often as I walked back and forth with my sign, I pictured my vacant office. I imagined my unattended mailbox. I visualized classes being held. If I was at a picket station that had access to faculty parking, I saw members of my own department, some few of whom had been friends, driving toward or away from their day's "ordinary" work. On Nineteenth Avenue I could see into the windows of my own campus building, where I might catch a glimpse of a colleague staring out at us. With a few rare exceptions, he became at once my enemy. If he had but recently come to the college, he was, in my mind, an upstart, a survivor at any price, a preemptor of what was mine, even an opportunist. If he had been at the college as long as I had, or longer, he was simply a traitor, or a coward. They were even moral thieves. They grabbed their paychecks at the end of the month for teaching on a campus that had been made safer and calmer by the picketing faculty lines, which striking students generally obeyed, thus keeping violence off the campus. And I, though still teaching in my home, was denied my check.

I had lived, I thought, almost all my life by reason and the distinctions it makes. By the first week in February, on the picket line, there was little of that left. In considering those who were not where I was—on the picket line—I lost my capacity to examine the two and three and four sides to everything. I reserved my distinctions for those who were on the picket line.

This anger deepened. I couldn't repress it. It was directed against all who were inside. I had never known I had such anger. It grew with every passing day and week of the strike, and all the more so as it became apparent that we were to gain nothing in any positive sense; we could at best claim we were controlling violence and sparing possible deaths. But that wasn't a positive claim; we couldn't prove it. And in the process of the picketing, then, I came to understand what the BSU leaders may have felt when they had so rhetorically, so absurdly, threatened us with gunslaughter if we taught our classes off campus.

There were moments when I thought I knew for the first time in my life what it was to think Black. It had nothing to do at bottom with arguments and rhetoric for justice, freedom, the *Little Red Book,* or any other book, or with Black is beautiful, or even with ten demands. It was simply the cry of "GIVE ME MINE!" And knowing, as you yelled, that you weren't going to get it. Not this time around. So the cry got angrier. And the anger went over your face like a sullen mask, like the portrait of paranoia, poisoning reason, blurring distinctions, giving spoiled food to hopeless fantasy. That, too, was perhaps a lesson of the body on the line: you know in your heart that you're going to lose. It keeps the anger up. And that might give you the one and only little freedom you have: the choice of style in which you lose.

The picketing, at first a six-hour stint, was eventually reduced to four. It could have left time for a routine and even productive day. But I was very much like a friend who had a crate of books sent to him when he learned he was to be stationed in the Aleutian Islands during the war. By the end of the year, he hadn't even opened the crate. The strike, and its picketing in the form of a daily march to nowhere, absorbed energy. Even away from the campus the strike imposed its environment.

The evenings were full of phone calls. An emergency meeting, a special arrangement for the picket line, messages received, some to be transmitted, calls from friends, or to them, exchanging the day's gloom or hope, speculations, prophecies, the inside scoop, the witnessed scene, and always the questions about the students: Are they getting anywhere? Are they going to settle? Is it all still nonnegotiable? And the rundown on colleagues: Isn't so-and-so remarkable? Can you really trust that one? Isn't this one a pain in the ass?

Yes. No. But. The phone, and the phone again. Often I was talking to Litwak, and at one point we thought our phones were tapped. Other strikers were positive about theirs, and we scoffed. But it reached the point in our own calls to each other where it was no longer reasonable to account for the clickings and the unpredictable functioning as a symptom of the general paranoia.

Outside of my family, my students provided ballast to my weeks. I continued to meet with them off-campus—as did many others of the striking faculty—and none of the Third World militants pursued us, or even threatened us, no less waved a gun. Almost all my students that semester were in the graduate program in creative writing. Some of them were in arrangements calling for individual conferences on their submitted manuscripts. We met in my home, gossiped about the strike, and discussed their fiction. On Tuesday evenings, a class of about thirty graduate students met in my home. We began at 7 P.M., as we would have on the campus, and for the first half-hour or so we talked about the college. On some issues they were unanimous: denunciation of the trustees, the chancellor, Reagan, scorn for Hayakawa. None of them expressed the belief—no matter how personally frustrated they were by events—that all things would have been better if the black students hadn't started anything in the first place, had waited, instead, for the good things to come their way. They agonized most about what they should do individually. Some of them put in a few hours on the picket lines. None of them would cross the picket line, and yet no one thought of himself as a political person. They identified with writers and literature, but most of them admitted that they weren't able to write now. A few of them wanted no grade for attending the classes, a price they wanted to pay because others were paying more. A few of the absent ones had dropped out of school for the semester.

I don't know whether our study of the texts of fiction was made better or worse for meeting in my home. The students preferred the change. The style as a "classroom" was certainly altered. We drank coffee and wine, and we proceeded through the evening—till midnight sometimes—in a mild aura of valor, a kind of self-congratulation for sticking to our vulnerable subject in difficult times. Discussion dominated. Lecturing in my own living room was impossible for me. I needed the institutional props to be comfortable with what is, after all, a kind of performance. The conventional setting allowed the lecturer-teacher to be a public man while it guarded his privacy. The paradox contributed to the authority many students wanted to undermine in the name of community. "I can't really answer you when you stand there in front of the room," that student had said to me in my office when he argued against term papers. There were times in these home classes when I valued the new intimacy. There were also moments when we talked Kafka and I heard my children upstairs or a neighbor's car door outside and had to ask myself: What were they all doing in my home talking about guilt and fathers and was Kafka really funny?

The strike, as it wore on, attacked my sense of will as well as my identity. As long as I had money left, quitting was impossible. But going on left me in the hands of others. I wasn't leading men but was being led, and if the good soldier role was necessary, it wasn't fulfilling. How long the role would go on was very much in the hands of the striking students. At depressed moments, that circumstance was painful. While I might believe, in times of anger, that I knew what it was to think like a Black, I never imagined I had become a Black. I might understand how far they thought they had to go, but I couldn't go there, and I resented being at the mercy of their needs. They couldn't gain the unconditional victory they had aimed at; the college was not about to accede to their ten demands. Nevertheless, I had to keep waiting for them throughout the faculty strike to say when they would quit the national spotlight and settle for such gains as they could get without threatening to resume violent tactics on campus.

And then there was Hayakawa. He continued, during the period of the strike, to be a master of provocation. He was always equal to the student rhetoric; there were times when he made amateurs of them. When he turned on faculty strikers, he intended his goading to be personal. Faculty strikers, he declared, were opportunists, cowards, frustrated writers, second-rate professionals bored with teaching. There was no way to answer him. He had the press interviews, the TV performances, the public—and the last word. Every reaction to him became grist for his mill. And what he intended personally, I took personally. But there was nothing I could do about it, except to remain on strike. And that determination began to run out in the form of another assault: money.

After the first of February, there was no way in my house to ignore the details of money. There was speaker's platform rhetoric, and café dialectic, and that stuff could go on till doomsday. And there was that other little detail: money. There were moments when I said to hell with the detail. I would use every last cent of savings before I would give in, and after that I would borrow from anywhere, and after that —well, we'd just see. And there were times when I dismissed such impulses as lunatic and had to confront some of the questions the lack of money implied. Would I have remained on strike past the first of February if I had used up all my savings by then? If I had had no savings when the strike began, would I have gone on strike? In the name of family bread, what was I willing to witness—or close my eyes to? If all the colleges and universities in the country should find their Hayakawa man, and if all the states should go the Reagan route, would I still teach? I couldn't earn dependable income any other way. Could circumstances compel me, too, to be "a good German"?

The students must have held the striking faculty in contempt for the money worries we began to express. In my twenties I might have shared that contempt. The students must also have felt the need to reassert their claim to the management of the strike. For too long, in their terms, they had walked the rim of the campus, obedient to our picket line. On January 23, they wanted their staging ground on the campus again, and they made no secret of it. The spectacle began sometime between noon and 2 P.M., shortly before I arrived for my shift of picketing. From my station on Holloway Avenue I caught glimpses, through the slots between buildings, of rushing students and squads of police. A colleague asked if I wanted to enter the campus with him and take a look. I refused. I had no desire to be arrested on behalf of the students' sense of what was tactically or emotionally necessary. I even resented the students for the violence they risked, thinking this time not only of them but of myself: so much of our cause in the faculty strike would fail if we couldn't prevent major violence.

Police made wholesale arrests. Blocking off exits from the quad, hundreds of police quickly encircled hundreds of milling students. The violence was minimal, the police maneuvers brisk. Through the afternoon we saw one van after another, marked with the police emblem and loaded with students, driving down Holloway Avenue. As late as 5 P.M. the vans were still leaving the campus. Through the small caged window in the rear door of one of them, a student, smiling, waved the peace sign. Then the van, as it went up the street, began to rock crazily. With grunts and cries we could hear in the street, the captured students flung themselves from one side of the van to the other. A solitary policeman, leaving the campus in his own car, slowed down when he came to our small picket line. He was quite human without his helmet—a warm smile, twinkling eyes, curly hair. "Did you enjoy your day's work?" one of the picketers asked him sardonically. But the young cop didn't ruffle. He smiled. He leaned his head out the window. "Three hundred and sixty to zero," he beamed. "That's not a bad score." He meant the arrests, and he had underestimated his victory. A total of 453 persons had been arrested on that afternoon, including a handful of the striking faculty who were most outspoken in their support of the student cause.

That was the last gasp of organized campus action by striking students. But there were still six weeks to go in the faculty strike, and no indication during that time that the student leaders would back off from their demands or that Hayakawa would help them to find a way to quit. On the first of March, the salary checks were missing again. The new spring semester had begun, and the administration ordered all faculty to meet their classes at the scheduled place and time or suffer the cancellation of the class.

That was it. I could go no further. More absurdity? More Kafka? I had played the academic game by all its rules for twenty years only to end up at a critical time with less power of protest than the kid welder at General Motors. Our own little strike brought home to me how little I had earned through the years in the way of real voice, no less rights. The only latitude left me now was to hang on for a few days, until the union itself voted to settle and return, sparing me the humiliation of doing it on my own. We had all but quit the

picketing and were meeting every day in emergency ses-
sions to discuss settlement. Our negotiating committee kept
reporting on its efforts with the four trustees who lived in the
Bay Area. Out of our yard-long list of labor complaints, two
concessions were offered. We would be assured of an improved grievance procedure on campus, and the striking
faculty who'd been separated from their employment would
be reinstated.

"It's a crock of shit!" cried one professor. Among us he had
always been the fiercest spokesman for unequivocal support
of the students in each of their demands. The vessels of his
neck bulged; his face was red. "If we accept those terms
we're worse off than we were before the strike. How the hell
can you do it to those kids?" he shouted. "How are you ever
going to look them in the eyes again? For chrissake, some of
them face jail sentences. How can you quit on them before
they get assurances of amnesty?" His voice cracked, the rage
penetrated by an hysterical despair.

Others spoke, declaimed, reasoned, shouted, mumbled.
Some were eloquent, some incoherent. Reasonable statements calmly presented were quietly received. The cries of
"Right on!" interrupted fiery speeches. Black student leaders
addressed us. One of them, without the *Little Red Book*,
without politically obvious rhetoric, talking in the humanistic
terms that could reach any vulnerable man, was utterly eloquent. He spoke with references to his own life, but the guts
of an American history was in every pause.

We started one of the meetings in the Buchanan Y. gym
early in the morning and went through the day. At noontime
wives arrived with huge pots of cooked food. The plates were
paper, the utensils plastic, the meal so-so, but the few moments of eating are richer now to my memory than any
faculty event I have ever shared. The fellowship of the strike

did have its moments of recreating for me what is perhaps the always indispensable kid stuff of life: the gang, the club, the fidelity beyond reason and possibility.

Our final meetings on the settlement hurt. Arguments against quitting the strike had an obvious power over me. They seemed to accuse me of being unable to bear what others were willing to. On the other hand, I thought they had gone crazy in their willingness. How could they dish out that stuff about betraying the students? We had bought them more than two months of additional time. If they had gained nothing for themselves during that time, they'd gain nothing if they had even more time. With the start of a new semester, the college could adjust to the loss of striking faculty. The blind need to assert will where there wasn't any power was a piece of futile heroics. I got angry all over again. What kind of frenzy had some colleagues in the union come to? Did they want to outdo Third World students in sacrifice and commitment? I got angry even at the eloquent black student leader. What if we did continue in the strike and the students settled two weeks after our classes were cancelled? We would be without jobs and pay until September, and they'd be back in school taking courses toward degrees. They could pledge now that they wouldn't do that, but they could tell us later we were victims of historic necessity. Right on!

At the union meeting to vote on the settlement issue, we lined up to turn in our ballots. I was voting to settle. I felt totally reasonable and, in the manhood sense, disgraced. The old question nagged at me as the line edged forward in the tense room: "Good German?"

We whispered, we engaged in small talk, we speculated about the outcome. Then a voice broke over us, shouting in anger. A young professor was pointing at someone on the voting line, calling out his name. He had discovered the president of the Academic Senate.

"What are you doing here? You got some goddamned nerve! How the hell can you show up here? And vote!"

"I'm in the union," came the calm reply. "That gives me the right to vote."

It was true. So remote must have been the possibility of a faculty strike to those who had formed the local and written its constitution that there was no provision in it for conduct governing a strike. All union members who paid their dues could vote, and no one who continued to pay his dues had been kicked out of the union for not joining the strike. The young professor was furious. He started scrambling over a few chairs.

"I've got a good mind to punch you in the nose," he shouted at the president of the Academic Senate.

"I wouldn't advise that," the older man replied calmly.

From a far corner of the room, a professor of philosophy joined in. "You bastard!" shouted the man who taught St. Augustine.

I glanced around the room and saw others who had not been on strike and had come now to vote an end to it. I also saw someone who was on leave and who would be financially unaffected by what we decided to do. I knew he was voting for us to continue. The president of the Academic Senate spoke to the people near him.

· "Of course I'm voting for you to settle. You're some of the best faculty the college has. The college can't afford to lose you. I want you back on the campus."

"Look," I said. "I'm voting to go back. I can't afford not to. I want the vote to go my way, but you're wrong. You shouldn't be voting. It was our strike, and it ought to be our vote."

He wasn't moved. In fact, he carried proxy ballots with him. He carried more than enough to make his one-shot appearance decisive. An end to the strike was approved by a margin of two or three votes. If the process of the strike had carried Kafkaesque overtones for me, the end of it was too blatantly absurd to be anything but foolish.

On March 18, twelve days after the end of the faculty strike, the students settled. They had been negotiating with a faculty committee even as their eloquent speaker had urged us to stay out. Their bind was not different from ours, except that it was, in the case of many of their leaders, more severe. They were exhausted and penniless, in some instances outright hungry. Funds of the Associated Students, which had supported them, were frozen. Out of all their demands, the crucial issue became amnesty. The revolutionary cause was reduced, understandably, to keeping the revolutionists out of jail. But the college could do nothing for those with criminal charges pressed against them by the police. The college wasn't willing to do much with some of its own charges. But the students, too, had to yield. And they had some last-minute drama of their own. To persuade their constituency to vote the settlement, some student leaders carried a tape recorder to the county jail where George Murray was being held for gun possession. They brought back his voiced approval of the settlement.

The students gained nothing they might not have gained without the war. The School of Ethnic Studies was established, but the administration, of course, retained control. There was to be no open admissions program for Third World students. Nathan Hare didn't get promoted; he was fired. George Murray didn't get his job back; he stayed in jail, his only permitted literature, as we heard it, the Bible.

I'm not wagging a finger at them. They went to war and

lost. They declared it by themselves for themselves. It was immensely preferable for them to the war in Vietnam where black men die for they know not what. About that Kafka could write a great deal. He could also write about the return of the striking faculty to the campus, the pickets of the rainy days back into the boss's shop.

11 · conflicting alliances

LEO LITWAK

My father organized the Detroit laundry and linen industry in the thirties, when the union business was rough-going. Hoods caught him on our front porch one night after a day on the picket line. They laid his head open and would have done worse if the neighbors hadn't interrupted. He went to the police station but couldn't identify his assailants. A few days later his car was stopped at an intersection, and he was dragged into the street and his teeth fractured. He bought a revolver, hired a bodyguard, left our house for the security of anonymous hotel rooms. He warned us to draw the blinds at night and to be careful not to offer silhouettes to snipers. We double-locked our doors and secured the windows. We were harassed by threatening phone calls. But his picket line held fast; he won his strike and our peace was restored.

I was proud of my father, though not always loyal. I marched with him during Labor Day parades. I could sing "Hold the Fort" and "Solidarity Forever" and "Pie in the Sky." But he exposed us to a risky life and there were times when I wished I could float anonymously in the mainstream like other kids. I was asked once—when I was ten years old and a new boy in school—to introduce myself to the class by telling who my father was. I listened to the other new boys recite enviable occupations—one father was a banker, another a mechanical engineer, another a tool and die maker. When my turn came, I identified my father as a "labor representative." Detroit being Henry Ford's home town, I hoped the class would assume that my father was on Ford's side of the fence, someone in personnel. Labor organizers weren't generally welcome in Detroit at that time. We studied Ford as if he were a god. We learned of his rise from humble Dearborn origins. We visited the mighty River Rouge assembly plant and Greenfield Village where the Ford memorabilia were on display. We were taught that Henry Ford had transformed the world. We celebrated the production line and the Model T and the eight-hour working day and the minimum wage and his other innovations. He had made America number one among nations. He had made Detroit number five among American cities. We owed our high standing to Henry Ford.

So organized labor was represented as a threat to us all, a corruption of the national character, a foreign import like fire ants or the corn blight. "Labor organizer" was often qualified by "pinko" or "commie" or "red." Foreign-born organizers like my father could anticipate the advice, "Why don't you go back where you came from?" That's the question a cop asked after arresting him for illegal picketing. My father had no intention of going back to Russia, where he'd been even less desired. At age sixteen he served a year in Russian prisons and Siberian exile. That didn't stop him from being a troublemaker in the new country. He named Ford for what he knew him to be—among other things, a bigot who had republished the "Protocols of the Elders of Zion," an anti-Semitic tract. He knew Ford as a vindictive union buster whose security chief, Harry Bennet, made free use of goons.

My father had no standing in the Establishment—he was foreign-born and vulnerable—and, nonetheless, he was undaunted. He said to the cop who advised him to return to Russia, "I'm a citizen who pays your salary. Arrest me; that's your right. But when it comes to my nationality, keep your mouth shut." He could speak up because he wasn't alone. He had the union behind him. He had Jimmy Hoffa on his side. The union was a prime source of his courage. It provided him with the backing to defy cops and to recognize the authority of his own needs and desires. I myself experienced—at union picnics and parades and picket lines—the joyful liberation of union brotherhood. The union *did* make you strong. It enabled workers to speak their minds to the bosses. It liberated them from an official morality that guaranteed the power of those who ruled.

During the Second World War, I came home on furlough from a Southern training camp, and my father took me to the second floor of Teamster Hall to greet Jimmy Hoffa.

"What do the GI's think of unions, kid?"

I told Hoffa it was my opinion that labor unions weren't popular among Uncle Sam's fighting forces. My captain, for instance, leading the obligatory discussion of current events, damned John L. Lewis and all striking workers as traitors, and that seemed a popular point of view.

In the cheeriest way, Hoffa said, "Screw 'em." He had nothing but contempt for anyone who could be bullied by officers or cops or judges. He was confident that once you gained power, the law would accommodate you. This defiance of established authority was part of Hoffa's charm. He worked out to keep in shape. He did push-ups in his office. A chunky, ruddy, big-chinned man, he saw the world as a battle ground and he meant to have a significant place there. A business agent once told me, "He may be a little guy, but he'll take anyone on. I saw him walk into a terminal full of scabs and ask, 'Who's tough here?' No one had the guts to speak up." Hoffa operated in the American grain, one of our top cowboys who muscled his own idea of justice into being. As for unpopular public opinion, he was confident that if you came out on top it could be reversed.

After the war, I spent a couple of weeks as an organizer for a Detroit union. I worked with two others. We stopped workers outside a plant and checked for union cards. Those without cards were asked to sign up at the union hall; otherwise we wouldn't let them through. I didn't have the nerve to forbid working men from entering the plant. But my companions could make their orders stick. One was a gambler from Toledo who operated an illegal casino. The other had just been released from a ten-year stretch in federal prison. He admitted—not without pride—that he had in his time committed every crime in the book, not excepting homicide. "But," he told me with relieving piety, "I never betrayed a union brother." While we waited for workers to arrive for the next shift, my colleagues discussed trade secrets. They brought out tire chains and demonstrated how best to swing them in a fight—with the open ends hanging free, if I rightly recall. They reminisced about famous local hoods. There was one who had outfitted a glove with an ice pick, but was more celebrated for his use of dynamite. The brief experience reminded me of the other possibility—which I had already learned during the war—that if established authority failed, tooth and claw would make the rules.

When my father—after expressing pleasure that I had become a college teacher—asked whether I intended to join a union, I answered, "Of course not." College teachers weren't like factory workers or truck drivers. The old slogans didn't hold for us. We didn't need a union to "make us strong." There was no question of "solidarity." It was every man for himself. Individual careers were founded on individual talents. Perhaps I worked for low wages, but by playing it right

I could get tenure and a guaranteed yearly salary and a three-month paid vacation, and best of all, no tire chains, or ice picks, or fractured teeth, or cut heads, or revolvers, or bodyguards, or threatening phone calls, or double locks, or fear of snipers.

When I saw the ad hoc committee picket the main entrance to campus, I didn't want to participate in their action and was irritated that I might be obliged to do so. These professors carried red signs that announced they were "on strike," but who were they kidding? They weren't laborers. They were English and psychology and sociology and philosophy and speech and economics faculty. How puny they looked alongside cops. Where were the burly teamsters and auto workers whose appearance made policemen reluctant to use their clubs? I only saw patrician ladies and professorial men and some exotic youths. It didn't look like a union picket line to me.

What did any of us have in common with the ordinary working man who put in an eight-hour day, five days a week, punched a time clock, worked under the scrutiny of a foreman, and received a mere two-week vacation? When the working man struck, it was for clearly defined and commonly accepted goals—higher wages, shorter hours, increased fringe benefits. Our professed goals were similar to these but were mainly intended to satisfy the Labor Council. We were actually striking for something more ill-defined and more revolutionary than the usual labor objectives. We knew that fundamental changes in higher education were necessary. And we had come to believe the problem of race on our campus needed a more radical approach than the Establishment had been willing to try.

These reservations were all beside the point. A few weeks

later I was on the picket line myself and voted to defy the court injunction which challenged the legality of our strike. The vote was unanimous. The union assembled at a synagogue two miles from campus and we marched back, carrying a forest of signs. Mine demanded faculty autonomy. I marched beside a woman who had been politically zealous during the Depression but had long since settled into academic grooves. Like me, she had suddenly awakened to the union cause. Once again we sang "Hold the Fort" and "Solidarity Forever."

Our picket line merged with the radical students. It stretched out to cover almost the entire front of the campus and half of one side, an extended, twisted ring. The Blacks had their own songs with improvised lyrics and jazzier rhythms. The rank and file picked up the verse from the picket captain and chanted the refrain.

The strike revivified a community fragmented by the design of careers. Our commitment had been to our own achievements and reputation, not to colleagues or to the college. We had negotiated with employers on the basis of our market value. We bore our grievances privately and guarded the small advantages we had over others. No longer. We were now united by the strike. For two months we walked the line together, and my colleagues assumed more than a professional dimension. The Chaucer man was also a carpenter, the classics man a film maker. The anthropologist had been a tail-gunner in the Second World War. The linguist was a mountaineer, the logician a swordsman.

Sharing common risks with my colleagues on the picket line gave me—for the first time in my academic career—a sense of fraternity I had always missed.

That's what I told my father in explaining our strike to him. I had resolved contradictory loyalties, and I was both an academic and a union man. At another time, I might have expected him to be delighted. I wasn't surprised that he had serious reservations about our strike, however.

He was visiting in San Francisco. He asked, What about a strike fund? Did we really think we could mount an effective strike without resources? Was it true that we had gone on strike with only a fifth of the faculty in our ranks? What kind of a bargaining position did we think we had? He couldn't understand the students' refusal to negotiate under such circumstances unless they were more interested in wrecking the college than in winning the strike. "Demand everything," he said, "but negotiate." He saw the process of negotiation as a test of power. You could finally achieve what was within your power, no more, no less. That the BSU refused to play the bargaining game confirmed his suspicions that their struggle was cloaked in the mantle of labor but had more radical objectives. He had always operated with the vision of union brotherhood as a model for the human condition. But after the Second World War his orientation to history was redefined by the Nazi extermination camps. The style of radical action had changed so markedly from his own time that he no longer could identify himself with radical causes. He mistrusted the dress, language, sexual behavior— the general theatricality—of the radical movement. He had never rejected bourgeois values *in toto*. On the contrary, he wanted them universally shared.

This opinion seemed to me common to labor men. It was undoubtedly one reason why so many of the Labor Council were reluctant to side with the faculty strike. They saw us march alongside young people whose dress was in itself a revolutionary act. The anomaly of our strike was obvious. We counted on the support of truck drivers while their leader, Timothy Richardson, tried to bring the San Francisco Police

Department within the teamster fold. Richardson organized a demonstration in front of City Hall to demand better living conditions for police. When young "hippy" types disrupted the demonstration, it was the teamsters who used their boots and fists to defend police honor.

I brought my father to our picket line, and before the day was over he discovered some enthusiasm for our cause. Dressed in a topcoat, wearing a tie, a hat, glistening black shoes, horn-rimmed spectacles, he joined the exotic parade of beards and hairdos and mod dress. Some Japanese faculty and students appeared in the guise of Samurai warriors. Braless girls marched in barely converted paisley bedspreads. A strumming troubador wore a black cape with red velvet lining. Third World students and their supporters wore red arm bands, Indian headbands, denim jeans and jackets. There were BSU picket captains with imposing naturals and Chicano leaders who resembled Castro and Che Guevara at their hairiest. Even professors were exuberantly costumed. They wore proletarian ponchos, sporty parkas from Abercrombie and Fitch, campaign hats, ski hats, Balaklava helmets, berets, sombreros. My father marched among a contingent of housewives from Marin County and students from Stanford and faculty from other campuses. He observed the ranks of police who stood between us and the campus, and he knew which side he was on. Perhaps you had to be there to know that.

The strike shook us loose from our anchorage and we found ourselves in a world no longer secured by tenure. We had an advantage over those who sympathized with us but refused to strike on the ground that ours was a losing cause. At least we were in motion, wrestling with our destinies, no longer satisfied to allow bureaucrats to decide our course. Our union headquarters had the exuberant informality of combat headquarters. Volunteers prepared sandwiches and hot coffee. Others worked Mimeo machines, readying strike literature. Here emergency funds were dispensed to needy faculty and reports were received from faculty on committee assignments.

For two months we were more than a faculty. The strike temporarily changed the quality of our lives. It produced a heightened consciousness which enabled us to experience brotherhood.

The students were never entirely reconciled to our strike. While they were able, with our help, to paralyze the campus, that was only incidentally their objective. They needed—in terms of their more radical goals—to keep up the momentum of their struggle, and this meant not allowing it to bog down in spirit-wasting routines. Their strategy depended on keeping those who had the power off balance. The state always had the means to smother the strike. It controlled the police and the money. The students had tried to create a snowballing effort that would appear suicidal and murderous if resisted. The sound and fury had been indispensable to their strategy, and the faculty picket line stifled that. It removed the action from the center of campus. And we faculty were law-abiding citizens, opposed to violence. Our strike was authorized by the Labor Council and, therefore, our picket line had a legitimate existence. Mayor Alioto had indicated he would not be party to breaking an authorized strike and refused to direct the power of the city against us. He had no such hesitations about the student strike. The cops were on familiar assignment at our picket line. They found us comprehensible animals. Not the students, however. "You people are okay," a young policeman said to me, "but not *them* animals." He nodded toward the front of the campus where students taunted cops and yelled obscenities.

The students gave the impression of being ready for martyrdom in behalf of a cause that transcended the local issues. They warned one and all that they'd blow up the place rather than return to their humble condition. And, indeed, a bomb that could have caused serious casualties was found behind a water fountain near Hayakawa's office. Another bomb did go off and shattered windows in the Administration Building. A fire bomb scarred the outside wall of the Administration Building. In the dying moments of the strike, the hands and face of a seventeen-year-old black student were shredded by a bomb that exploded in the Creative Arts Building.

We faculty made no threats to blow up the place. Relatively few of us considered martyrdom. Our cause was risky. We might be fired. But until the last, we still had options. We could, for instance, settle the strike, even though unfavorably, and wait for a more proper time to press our grievances. Hadn't we already achieved a great deal? We'd forged a community. The next time we could act in concert with fresh resources and greater numbers.

The Third World leaders urged us to continue the strike. Benny Stewart, chairman of the BSU, promised that the BSU would guarantee the job of any professor fired as a result of the strike. The BSU, he said, would not consider the strike over until every participant—student and faculty—was restored to his previous condition. Another BSU leader, Nesbitt Crutchfield, pleaded with us to stand fast. We had lost much, but consider, he said, what the students had sacrificed. They were entirely committed to the strike and there was no way out for them. Addressing a union meeting at the Buchanan Street Y.M.C.A. called to debate acceptance of a strike settlement, he told us that he had committed everything to the struggle. He had begun the strike with handsome Establishment credentials—an Air Force veteran, a business school graduate, a husband and father. Now he'd lost everything. He faced several felony charges, with the probability of serving a long jail term. Yet he would make the same commitment again. In the course of the struggle, Crutchfield said, "I became a man."

But we had come to the end of the road. By the end of the semester the administration realized that public opinion would support drastic action, and our own officers believed that if the strike were carried too far into the new semester we would be fired. Many of them favored a settlement. They saw our strike as a victory because it had created a militant organization. They told us that there would be future battles after we recouped our strength.

The student strike had also lost energy. The Third World leaders arrived with their minions in the afternoon and briefly swelled the union picket line. They took a few turns, chanted a few slogans, perfunctorily jeered the police, then departed.

When the time arrived for Hayakawa's presidential address, signaling the new semester, our strike had visibly eroded. Picket stations were unmanned. Absences at union meetings seemed to confirm rumors that many faculty had surrendered to the financial squeeze and signed their salary warrants and released their grades. I heard some union members discuss leaving San Francisco State. But the job market had already declined and S.F. State strikers were not welcome in most cases. Those without an academic reputation had no chance at all. I heard some half-heartedly consider other lines of work, everything from becoming longshoremen to bookstore clerks.

The presidential address at the beginning of the spring semester was Hayakawa's first appearance before a faculty assembly as the new college head. The proceedings were covered by television and radio. We wanted to demonstrate against this final legitimization of the man we regarded as a usurper. We didn't have much choice of strategy. He had demonstrated his genius for milking events for their publicity value. If we disrupted the speech, he would once again appear to be the feisty little guy who had successfully dared the bullies to do their worst. His gutsy performance would confirm a reputation that thrived on disruptions. He knew what the media wanted of him. We decided to actively boycott the speech. The union contacted the entire faculty, urging that everyone cooperate with us even if they had opposed our strike. They, too, could resent Hayakawa as the visible symbol of state power that had compounded our problems.

On the day of Hayakawa's address, we assembled in strength for the last time. We mounted a picket line that encircled the auditorium. It was the foulest day of the year —a hard, steady, cold rain fell with no prospect of a letup. But we recognized each other in foul-weather gear as we never had in academic garb. We cheered our leaders, we sang proletarian songs without embarrassment, confident that whatever loss we suffered, we had established our community.

The proceedings inside the auditorium were about to begin when Dr. Nathan Hare led black faculty members and administrators and BSU leaders through our lines. Some applauded as they passed through. I was perplexed that they ignored our line. They had evidently decided against letting Hayakawa survive his inaugural appearance without a protest being registered.

Our radios soon put us in touch with what happened inside. We heard shouts from the audience. I thought I recog-

nized Nathan Hare, among others, chanting, "Hayakawa got
no powah." Hayakawa ignored the interruption and began
his speech.

> Madam Chairman, Fellow Members of the Faculty—This is the
> traditional time for the president of the college to greet the
> faculty before the beginning of a new semester and to report on
> the state of the institution. I keep wondering, as I look at my
> notes, if this speech isn't going to be so much of a report as it is
> a form of prayer.

The heckling resumed. There were shouts of "Get off
the stage!" The radio commentator informed us that it
was indeed Nathan Hare who had led a group of Blacks
around the lectern, badgering Hayakawa with the chant,
"Hayakawa got no powah." We were told that the Tac
Squad waited in the aisles and in the vicinity of the stage,
ready to move in. For a moment the heckling subsided
and Hayakawa was able to proceed, continuing his reading almost breezily.

> Nevertheless, I am glad to be back at work. I have just spent a
> few days on the island of Maui, most of the time fishing from
> the deck of a motor sampan, the *Orion*, with a crew of ten
> native Hawaiians (Japanese, Portuguese, Hawaiian, Chinese,
> and one Anglo-Saxon), from whom I didn't hear a word of
> standard English for days. All we thought about was meals and
> beer and fish. I am fearfully sunburned all over, but I am cer-
> tainly rested and feeling fine.

This autobiographical small talk was amazing under the
circumstances. It claimed the kind of personal tone one
might expect from a sovereign. It flaunted his station and
his power and deliberately invited us to assume the posture of underlings.

So the howls started up again behind the stage. There
were countering shouts from the audience. The Tac

Squad moved in closer. When the flurry died down, Hayakawa resumed:

> On Wednesday morning in Maaleea Bay, we were fishing for bait, and I had a line out and started catching Opelu, a small Hawaiian fish. They were plentiful, and I was having a great time pulling them in one at a time. The captain saw the school of Opelu and decided we could do better. He ordered out a skiff and a hundred or more feet of net. With one end of the net on board, the skiff went out in a circle with the other end, and we began surrounding and catching Opelu not one at a time, but four hundred and fifty-three in a single sweep. The sight made me so homesick that I started out for San Francisco that night.

Obviously the reference was to the "big bust," when 453 students were netted. When Hayakawa began speaking of his vacation, I thought the subject so inappropriate that I imagined he either didn't want to speak frankly about campus affairs or that he was awkwardly trying to strike a personal tone which might win our sympathy. In fact, it was a needling reference, designed to provoke the striking faculty.

If we had been in the auditorium instead of outside, we would have provided the TV show Hayakawa had programmed. Nathan Hare and the BSU leaders obliged him. They refused to allow him to continue. The Tac Squad mounted the stage. Hayakawa, perfectly safe, his moment dramatically realized, shouted, "Get the hell out of here, Nathan Hare!" confirming the image he had so industriously contrived of a tough college president, able to withstand the most intimidating of black men.

The Tac Squad arrested Nathan Hare and a few others and ushered them out of the auditorium. Hayakawa—who did have "powah," derived from the governor and the trustees—went on to deliver what was intended as an inspirational address. After doing what he could to deepen divisions, exac-

erbate wounds, humble his opposition, he spoke in the mild
tones of a man bent on reconciliation:

> Monday the new semester begins. I urge everyone here today to
> enter the new term with resolve to serve the college you have
> chosen as your professional base. I urge you to keep up the fine
> work of inspiring and educating the wonderful young people who
> are enrolled here. I urge you to communicate with your fellow
> men to build the spirit of teamwork and cooperation that will see
> us through our difficulties into better days ahead.

The maudlin rhetoric was in contrast to the malicious act.
The man was so divided in his appearances and his utter-
ances that we could enter agreements with him only with the
greatest doubt that they would be respected. Yet there was
no alternative to settling with Hayakawa. We had exhausted
our financial resources. Our labor allies pressed us to accept
the offered settlement as the best we could get. Its main
feature was a new grievance procedure which offered some
protection from any punitive administration. There was also
an assurance that all faculty would be reinstated, without
prejudice, to their former status. The settlement could
hardly be represented as a stunning achievement.

Perhaps Nathan Hare didn't have options either. He saw
that our support would fail the Blacks and that both his strike
and ours would be lost. He had little to lose in defying
Hayakawa, since his tenure at the college was bound to be
short.

Hare subsequently expressed his bitterness in an article he
wrote for the Black Panther newspaper, in which he condemned the union as a group of opportunistic liberals, who
cashed in on a strike that was black-led and black-inspired,
who derived grubby advantage from the black sacrifices.

The picket line that we assembled to protest Hayakawa's
presidential address was in effect our last. We had stood fast

in a manner I never anticipated, taking risks American professors had never before dared. We had made steps toward a labor alliance. We had also made steps toward an alliance with minority communities. Unfortunately, these steps were not in the same direction.

The BSU always seemed to doubt our resolve, and there was a basis for their mistrust. They professed an irreversible commitment, while ours could be withdrawn with little consequence to ourselves. Reversion to our ante-bellum status would leave those of us with tenure relatively un-damaged. The militant students, however, had banked their academic futures on the strike and they held nothing in reserve. At least so they claimed. They had put their middle-class possibilities on the line and demanded that we do like-wise. But we had gone as far as we could.

12 · victims & persecutors

HERBERT WILNER

In the last days of our strike, I invited myself to lunch with a San Francisco member of the board of trustees. We had lunched once before, at his invitation, after he'd read my magazine article on the college. Though he was a corporation lawyer, he was anything but a table-thumping, cuff-linked, heavy-jowled trustee. He was tall, thin, tweedy—even a little rumpled—middle-aged and somewhat shy. He seemed a gentle person, a good listener, a man unmotivated by malice or political expediency. He was clear about the student and faculty strikes: he opposed them.

I went to this second of our lunches to speak against the rumored appointment of Hayakawa to permanent president of the college. It was self-indulgence, a chance to make myself heard by the one trustee I knew. He told me at once that Hayakawa would be the president; nothing could prevent the appointment. He implied what we all knew: after three months as a news-maker, Hayakawa could have of the trustees what he asked for. But the trustees wanted him anyway. Certainly the trustee I spoke to did. "Hayakawa restored courage to a city when it needed it." That was the approximate language he used.

I suggested that wasn't the point even if I could agree with the observation. When the college settled down in the time ahead to something more ordinary than warfare and head-lines, how would Hayakawa function? He had no administrative abilities; the major part of his responsibilities would probably bore him. The trustee smiled. He imagined

Hayakawa would go on with what he was doing now—travel around the country making speeches. Some other administrator would have the actual campus work. The trustee was obviously amused by Hayakawa's flair and told some stories. At one point, he moved silverware to show the physical arrangement of a trustees' meeting at which Governor Reagan sat at the head of a horseshoe table and Hayakawa sat opposite him at the open end. The Governor made a dramatic speech and Hayakawa, in full view of him, closed his eyes, dropped his head, and snoozed.

The trustee, having brought the scene back to his eyes again, laughed and laughed. I persisted. "If Hayakawa's appointed, it'll kill the college. As it is, we'll take five years to recover. With him as president—"

For the first time during our lunch the trustee was annoyed with me. My partisanship he might have understood, but my naïveté on behalf of it was too much. He rejected terminal rhetoric.

"He won't kill the college. No one can do that. Even someone who wanted to couldn't do that."

It is now, as I write, the beginning of the 1970 fall semester, about a year and a half since that lunch. The college isn't dead. Not to the outward eye and the unlying statistics. New buildings have gone up, go up. There's a third high-rise residence hall that was only an iron skeleton during the strike. A large addition to the library is almost finished, its windows facing the now unused speaker's platform from which Eldridge Cleaver insulted, threatened, wooed, and manipulated three thousand listeners. A nearly-completed life sciences building towers over Nineteenth Avenue. And there are still somewhat more than eighteen thousand students enrolled, and applicants are turned away. Only a handful of faculty has left the college by choice because of the

events of the strike year, and I'm told the English Department alone has received around a thousand applications for
the few positions to be filled. The college is still in San Francisco. The students are still sunning on the quad grass where
improvised crosses had once marked the bloodstains. A few
of the long-hairs toss Frisbees, and most of the girls are in
even shorter minis, and some are bra-less. Near the tree
grove on the main walk, young people sit at tables on which
their "life-value" wares are displayed for sale: crafted
leather, psychedelic candles, bio-degradable soaps, rings,
peace emblems. There are no political tables, and no political
banners, and I don't even see or hear of that toothless
preacher who used to holler in a gravel voice that politics
wasn't the way to the vast bosom of God. Indeed, all the
abrasive edges seem gone, vanished. Black students are less
apparently angry, and some even mingle with Whites.
Though there are not as many—how could there be?—black
students as the BSU had argued for through its demand of
open admissions, there are many more Blacks than were
here before the BSU made noise.

Indeed, that trustee with whom I had lunch can be my
guide now through the campus where I still work, and he
could say: "See—I taught you something about the nature of
institutions in our country. They don't get killed that easily."

I would have to say he was right. I would also say that
wasn't altogether what I meant. I didn't think the buildings,
or the students, or the faculty would go away.

And I begin to imagine how we might talk for a while, for
I haven't seen him since that lunch. Indeed, he's no longer
a member of the board of trustees. He was a Democrat, and
supposedly liberal, and his term was up and Reagan didn't
reappoint him.

"You mean," he might say, "there's leftover hostility

among faculty members? Well, that'll go away. Time will take care of it."

And I say, "Probably. But that's not the whole thing either." And he says, "You don't like the high-handed way Hayakawa runs things? But you didn't expect him not to gloat a little. You must have expected he'd make some of you swallow things. You have a personal thing about Hayakawa."

"I sure do. But that's not what I mean either. He won't be here forever."

"If you mean the hostility of the Reagan administration and of most of the people of California, you brought all that on yourself. Where did you get the idea that the government of California could stand for a minority trying to bully or blackmail it into closing a state facility?"

"From the same place Reagan got the idea when he closed all the campuses for a couple of days during the Cambodia and Kent State period. He was trying to maintain the public safety, he said. If that really was his reason, it matched what ours had been. But that's not yet what I mean. I mean that we're all hurt by what we learned in that year of the strike. About each other. About how we behaved, as a community, and one by one."

I guess I would have enough sense not to go on with it in this vein, not even to an ex-trustee. I would begin to sound professorial, mixing lectures with sermons. He wouldn't want to listen. It would sound to him like some old classroom of long ago, eye-opening for the moment, but inapplicable even by tomorrow.

Because for many of us, from the very beginning, the questions were strung out on the old moral line of the victim and the persecutor, and the distinctions to be made between these two designations. We couldn't help seeing it that way. Many of us teach subjects organized around these distinctions. They are sometimes terribly blurred distinctions, but if they were always clearly one thing or the other, we would not have gone on reading and discussing the great works produced by these confusions—not only decade after decade, but century after century. But if many of us on the campus had been almost precisely equipped to talk and talk and write about victims and persecutors, we were ill-prepared to act. Poetry can come out of rich confusions, but a hard action takes a rather limited clarity. At the very beginning of the crisis, some of us yelled "Strike!" and some yelled "Call the police!"—and my grandmother could have yelled either of these battle cries, and sometimes did, and she was a professor of nothing and could neither read nor write. She could hardly speak English, but those phrases came quickly to her tongue.

We learned among ourselves, during the crisis, what we always academically knew—that moral language is indeed for discussion and classrooms, and that the language of action is the language of power. Exerted sufficiently, power needs no language. In the face of power, we watched each other behave. We revealed ourselves, and our records are known to each other. We remember them. Those of us suffering from what Hayakawa called inflamed literary imaginations can project from what we remember into some unknown crisis of a future time that may have even deeper consequences.

I say again, then, that Hayakawa's appointment kills the college, but not because he is himself anything so particularly incarnadine. He's nothing but a little Kafka-funny token of how the power works. But he is the emblem of how we acquiesced and will keep on doing so. I don't mean only those who were on strike, for I learned also that that relatively small group, whoever they may individually be, is dispensable to the college and the state. It's the entire faculty—even those few who personally admire Hayakawa—who suffer him now, for he's the emblem of what real power can make us acquiesce to, now and at any time.

We are being told, for instance, that the right of grading our own students is only a privilege that can cost us our jobs if we don't deal out a sufficient number of C's so that the dullness of that grade will put forth in sufficient shine or shame all other grades. We are told that our recommendations for the appointments of deans and presidents are our privilege so long as our recommendations coincide with the desires of the ultimate agency of power. When they don't, the privilege is withdrawn and the time spent by and for the recommending committees is equivalent to that of any other parlor game, except for the lack of fun. We are told that the presidents of the colleges and the chancellor can cancel the engagement of any controversial speaker if, in his or their prejudgment, the speakers can incite to riot. We are told that faculty grievances are not to be settled by faculty committees, but by the president or the chancellor.

And all this kills the place because we acquiesce to it. More than that, it makes many of us look ahead to what other privileges will be shorn off and punishment imposed. Cuts in budget? A freeze on salaries? Increase in teaching loads? Cutbacks in promised programs? Well, that's already happened. And we acquiesce. And if they legislate what we can teach in the classroom, and how we choose to teach it? Will we acquiesce then? Of course we will. Because we learn every day to acquiesce more and more, and the shame of it gets blunted. But flattening shame doesn't make it disappear. And that too kills the place. Because a good number of us still teach subjects which have moral distinctions at the center of their content, and now we share a common campus experience that tells us how those distinctions stop where power begins. Maybe we ought, then, to be leading discussions about power apart from moral distinctions. But most of us won't ever do that. Our lives are in our subjects and in moral distinctions. Only our fates are in the hands of power. And that kills us too. In our penny-ante games, we don't know very much about power, or our fates.

Maybe we are finally at San Francisco State, as a faculty, in that place where some of the students thought they were when they began this mess. If they were, indeed, the ones who began it. They stopped talking about moral distinctions and talked about power. In one way they were like some of their professors—at least their leaders were. They often talked as though they understood everything, but they acted with a passionate innocence. They had no power ultimately to take on the power they were after.

But I can't begin to talk about the students without getting into that old line of the victim and the persecutor, and that's a return to the moral language. For the black man, en masse, has always been a victim in this country. Awesomely so. But who is to say how the victim shall behave in behalf of his liberty or in some delusion for his liberation? Shall his persecutors be his guide? Anyone with a clear answer to this question in all living situations knows a lot more than I do. Some even profess to know the answers in advance of the situations. I only know a long list of other questions.

At what point does the victim, attempting to liberate himself, become a persecutor? Who is to judge these indentifications, rightly or even accurately? Is an individual who belongs to a social class of victims to receive compassionate understanding when he acts out his anger? How is this understanding to be managed in the face of the overriding need for social order? If it is true that all persecutors have victims, but all victims don't have identifiable or accessible persecutors, is the persecutor to be identified by the victim only? Is symbolic action by the victim justified? Does it matter to what degree someone is a victim or a persecutor? Who is to identify the degrees? Who is to dictate the terms of social change when the victim doesn't have the power to do so and the persecutor or the "neutral" doesn't have the same pressing desire? Can a nation of laws that are generally just tolerate the disorder that is the consequence of its own unjust application of the laws? Is there any value in general answers to these general questions without the facts of their concrete instances?

The situation at San Francisco State evoked all these questions, but only those people, especially at the beginning of the process, who thought themselves to be purely victims, or who were purely political, or purely simple-minded, could believe they had the certain answers. For many others—surely for myself—today's perception was tomorrow's revision. The assertions and their cancellations went even from hour to hour. The juggling produced a painful anarchy of mind. Sometimes, role-playing for relief, I entered imaginary dialogues with a black student leader. But I never got the best lines.

"There's a better way of accomplishing it," I said to him, and he said, "How?" and I said, "By going through channels because . . ." and he rolled his eyes and said, "Ha ha."

I said, "In the long run you're going to hurt yourself this way," and he said "How *long* is that?" I said, "Long enough to set back the very things you want to get," and he said, "Look, when did I ever have the things I wanted to get?"

"Destroying typewriters. Intimidating students and faculty, most of them on your side until you started that. It can only end with your bringing the cops out here. They'll be all over the place."

And he said, "That's fine. Let them do their work. They can do better for us than we can do for ourselves. Then we'll see where you are."

And always I finally said, "If I were president of this college, and even if you had gone through channels, and even if I had the power to grant them, I wouldn't accede to all your demands."

Always he would stare at me then for a long time, and he would nod, and a look would fill his face that was something between pride and cunning. But he wouldn't answer me. So I would be led to speculate if that look wasn't the very reason for his making such demands nonnegotiably.

And sometimes, even now, I resume that conversation with the defeated leader, and I say, "See. I told you. You got less than you would have had if you'd gone through channels. And look at the mess you've left behind."

And he says, "So at last you drop all that moral stuff. Finally, you ask me a political question. You're talking win and lose. Funny thing. I suppose you know what happened not long after our thing, way on the other side of the country at CCNY. Another campus scene. What they call unrest. Racial content, you would say. Lots of cops. Blacks fighting with Whites. Campus closed a long time. Well, you know what I mean. They got open admissions there now. And that was one of our demands that stuck in your throat, wasn't it? What do you suppose then? Here's this CCNY with all that tradition of high averages, book-grinders. You suppose they got fired up with a moral enlightenment you can't begin to see at San Francisco State? Or you suppose it's a little because CCNY sits right there in Harlem? And Harlem has some day-by-day power when it comes to saying that's going to be a peaceful campus or a wild one, cops or no cops. There's no use, you see, us talking about moral dilemmas. Do you want to talk a while about power? Let me hear again what you got to say about this business of governor, chancellor, trustees, faculty. You dig?"

"Of course I do. We *are* talking about the same things, then. Making some of the same distinctions."

"We are? I didn't hear any of that."

"You just admitted you didn't have the power here to bring off what you wanted."

"Hell, man! You're part of why we didn't have it. You and your faculty strike. What did you want out of it except for us to go away? You threw up your picket line to take us away. You taught your classes at home to take your students away."

"Of course I did. I'm not going to apologize for that. What did you think I'd do? I'd do it again that way, if I'd do it at all. You still have to answer the unavoidable question. Do you believe you can make victims of all of us just because you're a victim? Do you think the witness is always just as guilty as the perpetrator? Do you think . . ."

Now, whatever the setting I've imagined for our dialogue, he turns his back on me and begins to walk off the stage of my mind. He is shaking his head as he leaves, and when I call him back, he turns for his last words. They're always the same.

"Man, you're back where you began. You can't be taught what you ain't disposed to learn. And that's what you started out hollering about. It's getting too rough to teach *your* subject, you hollered. And I said, at the beginning, 'How rough do you think it is living mine?' And now there's getting to be a lot more of me than just me. White niggers and all. You dig?"

13 · old myths & new: the aftermath

LEO LITWAK

Jack Alexis, the BSU leader who instructed faculty and students on the revolutionary objectives of the strike, was deported to the West Indies.

Nesbitt Crutchfield—the moderate voice of the BSU who once implored the faculty not to yield, confessing that the strike had cost him all he owned—was convicted of arson and spent a year in the county jail.

Jerry Varnado—the militant BSU leader who described himself and his comrades as "madmen, terrorists in behalf of freedom"—served a term in jail and enrolled in law school.

Benny Stewart, chairman of the BSU, enrolled in law school.

George Murray—cause célèbre, Minister of Education of the Black Panther Party, whose call for guns aroused the entire state—was in solitary confinement during much of his six months in prison. He renounced violence, quit his ministry with the Black Panthers, and enrolled in the Stanford Graduate School.

The Chicano leader of the Third World Liberation Front became a carpenter and attempted to organize Chicano workers.

The black deans and administrators either resigned or were terminated.

Professor Juan Martinez, a faculty spokesman for the TWLF, services terminated.

Professor William Stanton, organizer of the faculty ad hoc committee, refused tenure by President Hayakawa, services terminated.

Russell Bass, president of the student body, left college, became a staff member of the *Whole Earth Catalog*. He turned toward Yoga and communal living and away from politics.

The Economic Opportunities Act Program was reduced in size and hedged with restrictions to prevent radicals from drawing sustenance from it. As punishment for campus turmoil, the state legislature denied faculty members the cost of living salary increase awarded to all other state employees. Criminal statutes were introduced that penalized students barred from campus if they tried to return. The radical students were no longer visible. Many served jail sentences and left college. A few returned to college for their degrees, seemingly dispirited but back on track. Others carried their politics into the ethnic neighborhoods. Some dropped out entirely in favor of communal life in the countryside.

The wave of rebellion subsided and the institution reappeared, unmarked. Though new buildings had gone up, the campus seemed shabbier. Food services deteriorated as the campus was sharply affected by the economic recession.

Chancellor Dumke was more sovereign than ever. He could appoint college presidents without consulting local faculties. In defiance of the strike settlement, the trustees made him final arbiter of all grievances, even those he had initiated. In some cases, he overturned the judgment of college presidents and boards of appeal.

New trustees were appointed by Governor Reagan and the revised board more closely reflected his vision and attitudes.

President Hayakawa exercised far more authority than his recent predecessors. He defied faculty opinion in his choice of deans. He set aside departmental retention and tenure decisions when they did not suit him. Many of the A.F.T. leaders were dismissed.

The A.F.T. itself lost effectiveness. Attendance at union meetings diminished until only the original faithful were left. The local chapter was eventually absorbed into a new faculty organization with powerful statewide representation.

The anti-strike faction received its awards:

Professor John Bunzell survived the harassment of the BSU to become president of San Jose State College.

Hayakawa's executive vice-president, Professor Jones, became acting president of Sonoma State College.

Other Hayakawa supporters filled the administrative ranks of San Francisco State College.

I draw up this tally reluctantly. It seems to offer a list of winners and losers, with the strike faction on balance totally routed and the forces represented by Hayakawa and Reagan entirely victorious. I have qualms about this sort of calculation. George Murray, for instance, may have emerged from profound changes a more extraordinary person. The BSU leaders may have had to take the journey they took, and perhaps are better men in consequence. Impossible calculations would have to be made before I could judge who won and who lost. A decade from now we may realize that the faculty members who were fired were better off than those who stayed.

I didn't myself want to defeat anybody. I didn't favor an unequivocal BSU victory, since I couldn't support the fifteen demands. At the same time, I didn't want the BSU defeated. I hoped the struggle would in the end unite and revitalize our campus. As for myself, I saw the possibility that the contradictions of my life on campus and my life away from it could be resolved. There were days on the picket line when I felt whole again, no longer divided by contradictions.

Yet, however I might have wished, the game terminated with losers and winners. Two years after the strike, San Francisco State College had the ambience of a defeated land. It had been for a time one of the most vital places in America, inviting the changes that revolutionized the sixties. It ended up a battlefield.

One of the consequences of seeing the strike as a "battle" to be won or lost was that it became necessary for both sides to cast the struggle into terms that misrepresented it. For instance, I heard a professor of journalism, early in the strike denounce the student radicals as Nazis. "I fought against them in World War Two," he said, "and I'll fight them here and now."

Reagan and Hayakawa pointed to the similarities between our local revolutionaries and Hitler youth. Both shouted you down when you tried to be heard. Nazi youth and revolutionary youth pumped their right arms into the air. The chant, "Shut it down!" had the same effect as *"Sieg heil!"* Hayakawa identified himself as a long-time Nazi fighter. He considered the book that made him famous, *Language in Thought and Action,* a blow against Hitlerism.

A former University of California administrator, once regarded as a militant, urged me to stand against the student strikers. It was his opinion that the battle for San Francisco State was being studied throughout the country. It was a battle that higher education dared not lose. The strike had to be crushed even if San Francisco State were destroyed in the process. No appeasement. The revolution had to be stopped on our campus before it spread to Berkeley and Stanford and Harvard and the other places that mattered. He didn't doubt that the effort mounted at State was an escalation in campus rebellion that had nationwide implications. The pattern would be set for all other activists. For the first time, there had been attacks on the academic person and destruction of academic property. Bombs had been used. Hadn't we learned the lesson of the German universities? He conceded that Hayakawa wasn't his idea of a scholar or an intellectual and his presidency might even be the death of us. Nonetheless, he was behind Hayakawa all the way. The line had to be drawn at S.F. State. "Better Hayakawa," he said ominously, "than the man who will come after him if he fails."

Hayakawa, following the governor's prescription, did stand fast. He did find a way to solve campus disruption, and as a consequence, diners applauded him when he entered restaurants. He was honored by the Tac Squad "second platoon" at a private dinner. The solution he found was represented by a gift cigarette lighter sent him by a Marine outfit, displayed in his office. It bore the motto, "Grab 'em by the balls, and the heads and hearts will follow."

That's a hard prescription, but what choice is left when you are under Nazi attack? Hayakawa and Reagan argued that the struggle wasn't about racial injustice or academic reform. Our way of life was being threatened; democratic process was being imperiled. No one should imagine that these students were merely high-spirited kids. They were convinced revolutionaries, using Nazi tactics, and there was no alternative to a police solution.

What marred the analogy was that the students based their

own actions on the same lesson of history. They claimed that the Nazis were on the other side. They denounced "fascism," and spoke of genocidal policies, and constantly warned that "We ain't gonna march into gas chambers like good Jews." They damned those of us who were neutral, accusing us of being "good" Germans. They argued that being "good" would facilitate the perpetuation of the "trick that's been played on us for three hundred years." To be "good" in an oppressive system meant to conspire in your own murder, as was the case with the "good Jews," or to collaborate in the murder of others, as was the case with the "good Germans."

The opposing sides named each other "Fascist" and "Nazi" and shouted "No appeasement!"

It's true that these radical students assailed a way of life, but how could they be called Nazis? They urged "power to the people." They claimed that they wanted every man to be able to choose his own destiny. They opposed bureaucratic authority. Their meetings were models of democratic action. When they called for guns and used force to prevent classes from operating, they had to justify the departure from their utopian vision on the grounds that they were engaged in a revolutionary struggle against a fascist oppressor. They attributed to their opposition the murder—psychic and otherwise—of ten generations of black people.

While they presented a strong case against the system, they failed to prove that their enemy was fascist. One need only consider the tally at the beginning of this chapter to see that the charge is a distortion. The state didn't wipe out the strike leaders who survived their punishment to become aspiring lawyers and businessmen. Most of the striking faculty members were fully reinstated.

There was nothing fascist about Reagan's vision. It was grounded in American myths. He regarded himself as an egalitarian. He deplored bigotry. In his autobiography he described how his father refused to stay at a hotel that would not accept Jews. He himself encouraged Negro athletes when professional sports were first segregated. He regarded such actions as evidence of his good will. While he opposed government legislation in the field of civil rights, it was out of fear of enlarging the scope of government. He warned of creeping socialism. Loss of freedom was, he believed, the inevitable by-product. His vision was that of a small-town boy who remembered his own Huck Finn childhood with nostalgia, and cherished the memory—or the myth—of a serene America, thrifty, tidy, healthy, mannerly, industrious, and number one in everything.

Both revolutionaries and Establishment claimed a view of human possibility which they suspended in the face of the enemy. They paid lip service to democracy and operated instead as if their morality were derived from cowboy movies. The Panther lingo, used by the BSU and its cohorts, was an amalgam of insult and Marxist jargon. The struggle might be presented as a war between the exploited and the exploiters, but when passion infused the language, the attitude was not that of a scientific socialism. The tone was Homeric. Or Arthurian. Or American cowboy. Cleaver threw down the challenge. Reagan picked it up. His own vision was deeply shaped by his sporting experience and his cowboy roles. He believed in going all out for his team. He was an effective president of the Screen Actors Guild. He helped root out Hollywood subversives in the days of the blacklist. He was a long-time warrior against atheistic Communism. Addressing a meeting of the Full Gospel Businessmen's Fellowship International, he was quoted as saying that our society approached a crossroads.

"Very shortly we will either turn and go down a wrong

path or turn and go in another direction, and we're going to see one of the greatest spiritual revivals of all time."

In 1965, as Reagan was about to enter the gubernatorial campaign, I interviewed him for the *New York Times*. I watched him address a Lions Club meeting, a graceful, powerful, bronzed man, with the precise definition I've noticed in other actors, as if their design is partly due to a haberdasher. He delivered an enthusiastically received speech in a tone that had a decidedly rural cast. "A government is like a baby. What you put in one end of the alimentary canal comes right out the other." He told of absurdities that resulted from crop quotas imposed on farmers. The audience of doctors, lawyers, and politicians adored him. I had been informed that the speech so fluently delivered had been years in the making. When his movie career petered out, he began a new life on television for General Electric. Driven by the team spirit, he mastered the free enterprise argument in hundreds of appearances at GE plants. Democratic policymakers were eager to get Reagan into the campaign, believing that he would be totally inept when he had to depart from his canned speech.

Two hours with Reagan convinced me otherwise. He indeed had the simple, homespun faith of the small-town boy when he addressed his own folks. But off-stage he was far more than that. He could read his interrogator quickly, guess his attitudes and his point of view. He was in an instant persuasive, combative, thoroughly the master of his position. He may have been ideologically naïve, but he was quick on his feet and had a powerful attack.

He wasn't a man to refuse challenges. He was ready for shoot-outs. He wasn't intimidated by the revolutionary threat. He was only irked that others took it seriously. He scorned the cowed faculty and irresolute administrators who were buffaloed by the revolutionary theater. He knew an act when he saw one. He'd acted in enough cavalry charges himself to recognize that Indians with bows and arrows didn't stand a chance against the armed forces of the state. And yet, if he disparaged the firepower of these self-styled revolutionaries, he didn't ignore their ideological potential. His own vision of America was under assault, not only from these militants, but from the Left generally; in fact, from all those forces that accepted the bounty of a welfare state.

I understand Reagan's great popularity when I see him as the standard-bearer of a mythic America, fashioned in schoolrooms and in movie theaters. When Reagan went to Hollywood, he yearned for Western roles. He wanted to ride a horse. After a series of reluctant performances as fast-talking newsmen and Shirley Temple's first screen lover and Bozo the Chimp's attendant, Reagan finally became a cowboy. The role swallowed him. Inside the semblance of a hawk-eyed gunfighter was a near-sighted man who wore contact lenses. Inside the semblance of a warrior was a man who spent the war years as a Special Services officer in Hollywood.

But when the country needed a good guy to manhandle the villains, Reagan had been trained for the job.

Is it too absurd to argue that our childhood dreams of cowboy justice influence our antagonisms and our competitions? The cowboy myth is too powerful to be confined to movie theaters. Americans have proved they are ready to elevate their pretend cowboys to high office, presuming, with good reason no doubt, that the role which has been performed again and again has established habits which will survive when the cameras stop rolling.

There was no reason for Reagan to doubt what he pretended to be. Consider the more imposing case of his buddy,

John Wayne. John Wayne never killed anybody. Nobody ever killed John Wayne. And yet we credit him with a history in which he has slaughtered armies and has died often enough himself to have been a squad. He stands beside Governor Reagan in campaign photos and the voice that rallies us is the voice of a veteran who has survived Normandy, Iwo Jima, the Red River, the travails of being a frontiersman, a cavalry officer, a cowhand, a cattle baron, an Indian scout, a Marine, a sailor, a pilot.

During the war, I saw John Wayne storm a Pacific isle and wondered, for a moment, why this extraordinary soldier wasn't in the real action. Perhaps he created a necessary illusion that our history had form and direction and that if we kept on fighting we'd gain paradise. Consider my slovenly, ill-designed battlefield in Germany. No one would ever have a clear view of its order. The generals were limited to maps and aerial photos and intelligence reports. It would take a god to view the entire battlefield. Who else could see in a single glance men hit by shells in the foreground, others nearby digging slit trenches, others snoozing or eating K rations or reading hometown newspapers? Tiger tanks maneuver on the other side of the valley. Miles away we see camouflage nets over artillery positions. Phosphorous shells ignite the horizon and ancient villages are skeletonized. That's a god's-eye view. What I in fact saw was the ground I hugged in my arms. Hollywood gave me the vision reserved for Homeric gods. I shared the vantage point of John Wayne, who was able to comprehend an entire battlefield.

And so, taking the shapeless battlefields of history, Hollywood provided a form. John Wayne and Ronald Reagan, among others, enacted fictions about the Old South and the Wild West. Sometimes they wore gray uniforms, sometimes blue. They operated within the moral limits of the Hays office and a generation of Americans understood the history of the nation within a fictional context designed by childish minds. These movies, though purported entertainment, were really an indoctrination. The size of our world was defined by Hollywood. The actor was as deluded by his fiction as was his audience. There was every expectation that he could step out of the screen and provide the form that the world seemed to lack. He was armed with integrity and courage and his trusty shooting iron.

Reagan came to office in the aftermath of the Free Speech Movement, prepared to restore the proprieties that most Americans believed should govern the campus. He had offered tough council and the public was ready for cowboy ways. He wasn't about to be intimidated by academic intellectuals who had the mistaken notion that the Golden Land belonged to them. When he was warned that his efforts to squeeze the fat out of the colleges and universities might lose Berkeley some of its Nobel prize winners—it was number one in that commodity—Reagan was ready to see them go. He would rather have zealous teachers, eager to do a full day's work, than arrogant intellectuals who wanted a soft life at the state's expense. He announced that it was his hope that the colleges and universities would correct their pronounced liberal bias through more selective hiring. He expressed a disenchantment with academic politics and academic reputations and academic giantism. He was far more eloquent than college bureaucrats, who seemed to have no greater vision than augmenting their empires. Reagan appealed to the taxpayer. Property taxes soared out of hand. The state budget swelled each year and education and welfare devoured the major part. Why shouldn't professors put in an honest day's work instead of aiding the enemies of the state?

He reflected the mood of the public. My garageman, for

instance, quarreled with me throughout the strike, trying to convince me that I had been misled. He gloated over the busted heads and the jail sentences.

"What do they expect?" he asked. "They're gonna smash windows and throw bombs, then let 'em suffer. No salary increase for professors? That's letting 'em off easy. Fire the bastards. Kick 'em out. When they learn respect, then they can come back. Let 'em go out and work for a living." He would just as soon see the whole show close down. He wanted the campus purged of all those who had profaned the dream. It was his dream as well. He didn't want street and campus made homogeneous. The intrusion of one place on another bothered him. What did it all mean if some wild-haired kid wearing a headband and an arm band and dirty jeans and cowboy boots called the college president a "motherfucker" and a "pig" and wasn't struck down on the spot and flogged until he begged for mercy?

My garageman was in the war. He may have been on the front lines and perhaps suffered far more than I did. He surely returned to no heaven. He told me that he barely scraped through the fifties, working as a mechanic and a truck driver. His pennies came the hard way. And rough times faced him once more. His service station had to compete with the one down the block and another two blocks away. The oil companies had forced an increase in gas prices during depressed times. He feared that his customers would cut down on gas consumption.

He works hard and still goes to movies on a weekend night. He has kept the faith despite the experience of war, despite living in the city where the drug scene had its origin, as well as psychedelic music and beatniks and hippies and student revolutionaries. He has two children almost ready for college. They will have an opportunity he never had. They may try to go to San Francisco State College.

He hoped that with the crushing of the strike at San Francisco State and the smothering of revolutionary movements life would return to normal. Yet everything has changed for the worse, he feels. He blames the revolutionary youth for having spoiled the sweetness of life. They made Hollywood laughable with their spirit of camp. When he goes to a Saturday night movie and puts down six dollars, hoping to be captured by the same illusion that has salvaged each week of his life, it's not there any more. It's undone by the bearded kids who laugh at John Wayne and Ronnie Reagan. He looks into a poster store and sees Reagan dressed as a cowboy with a gun in hand. He reads in the newspaper about a cowboy movie made with fag cowboys and the idea both shocks him and makes him smile. He sees war movies that ridicule America and celebrate malingerers. He turns around and doesn't notice anyone shocked and settles down himself to watch uncomfortably. He has less tolerance for cowboy movies. He feels that he is changing and he's depressed.

He was one hundred percent behind Hayakawa and the cop swinging the riot stick. He wanted judges to sentence revolutionaries without mercy. That's happened and yet it's not been set right. He is troubled by his own fickleness to what he once regarded as unalterable proprieties. His youngest children will soon be released into the world. And they are good children, but with far less reason than he to be faithful to the old vision.

He has misgivings about Reagan. The governor sounds great and he looks great, and doubts vanish when he reminds you of the common vision. But my garageman is not wholly sympathetic to the governor's belief that a college education is a "privilege," not a "right." That's fine if it keeps the lazy troublemakers off campus. But how about his kids who are

C students even though they study hard? He doesn't want them excluded from the aristocracy that has opened up to everyone else. The new tuition fees and the Spartan education budget worry him. And sometimes he experiences a nightmare more profoundly disturbing than anything that happens on campus or on the street. He dreams that the Great Depression has returned and all the gains of the past thirty years have vanished and that in his middle age he's again as vulnerable as he was in his childhood.

He lacks the satisfaction that goes with winning. He asked me how things were at San Francisco State. "Depressed," I told him. "There is no spirit to the place. It's as dull as a grave."

Good, he said. Fine. The quiet of the grave suited him. And yet he showed no evidence of satisfaction. The world hadn't been set right by his victory at San Francisco State. Those black students and their radical white allies have spoiled the fiction. They have taken up the cause of the Indians and the Chicanos and the Blacks, and they have damned the Hollywood version of American history as a lie, and now the old movies are a bore. It becomes increasingly difficult to revere cowboys in whatever guise they assume.

And for those of us who remain at San Francisco State there is a like problem. The war is over and we can't recover the feeling of normalcy. The BSU had warned us that things would never be normal again. But they were defeated and those boasts seemed empty. I was relieved that the strike was over because I, too, hankered for normalcy. I wanted to recover my detachment, divide my life again into that part which teaches and that part which is concerned with cardinal matters. It can be done, but no longer protected by self-delusion. The quadrangle has been re-sodded. Students laze on the grass. But we can't forget that this place has been violated and was once a battlefield. No matter how deaf we make ourselves, we can still hear the sounds of the street.

Those extraordinary days of 1968 revivified us. We all experienced that roller coaster excitement that Hayakawa enthusiastically reported. We are weary in the aftermath of those days. We don't want them back. Yet it becomes clear that the final tally has not been made. The victory of worn-out myths that no longer beguile even children is only temporary. Our black mentors forced us to become aware of the contradictions we had managed to evade, and we can no longer pretend that we are innocent. The old dream is gone. We await something new.

About the Authors

LEO LITWAK was born in 1924, in Detroit. He was educated at Wayne State University, the University of Michigan, Columbia University, and the New School for Social Research. He has taught at Washington University in St. Louis and at Stanford University. He is presently a professor on the faculty of San Francisco State College.

Mr. Litwak's articles and stories have appeared in such magazines as the *New York Times Sunday Magazine, Look, Partisan Review, Esquire, Midstream,* and *Commentary.* He received the Longview Foundation Award for his story "All Men Are." His story "In Shock" received the National Endowment for the Arts Award. His stories have appeared in the O. Henry and Martha Foley annual selections. He is the author of two novels, *To the Hanging Gardens* and *Waiting for the News,* and was awarded the Edward Lewis Wallant Memorial Book Award and the Jewish Book Council of America Award for the latter novel. In 1970 he was a Guggenheim Fellow.

Mr. Litwak has one child.

HERBERT WILNER was born in 1925, in Brooklyn. After graduating from Brooklyn College and Columbia University, he attended the University of Iowa, where he received his Ph. D. He has taught at Yale University, the University of Iowa, the University of Kansas, and the University of Innsbruck, the last as a Fulbright Visiting Professor. He is presently a professor on the faculty of San Francisco State College.

Mr. Wilner is the author of two books, *All the Little Heroes,* a novel, and *Dovisch in the Wilderness,* a collection of short stories. His novel was awarded the Gold Medal Prize in Fiction of the California Commonwealth Club. His stories, which appeared in *Esquire,* the *Saturday Evening Post, Sewanee Review, Epoch,* etc., have been reprinted in the O. Henry and Martha Foley annual selections.

Mr. Wilner is married and has three children.